Becoming American, Becoming Ethnic

In the series
Critical Perspectives on the Past,
edited by Susan Porter Benson, Stephen Brier,
and Roy Rosenzweig

Becoming American, Becoming Ethnic

College Students Explore Their Roots

Edited by Thomas Dublin

Temple University Press Philadelphia

Temple University Press, Philadelphia 19122

Published 1996
Printed in the United States of America

∞ The paper used in this publication meets the requirements of the American National Standard for Information Sciences—Permanence of Paper for Printed Library Materials, ANSI Z39.48–1984

Library of Congress Cataloging in Publication Data

Becoming American, becoming ethnic : college students explore their roots / edited by Thomas Dublin.
p. cm. — (Critical perspectives on the past series)
Includes bibliographical references.
ISBN 1-56639-438-4 (cloth : alk. paper). — ISBN 1-56639-439-2 (pbk. : alk. paper)
1. Ethnicity—United States. 2. College students—United States—Family relationships. 3. United States—Emigration and immigration. I. Dublin, Thomas, 1946– . II. Series: Critical perspectives on the past.
E184.A1B33 1996
305.8′00973—dc20 96-3554

To My Students over the Years
in History/Third World Studies 7B
and History 264

Contents

Acknowledgments

This volume has taken shape over an eighteen-year period and has benefited from the assistance of numerous individuals over the years. First, I thank the students I have had in History/Third World Studies 7B at the University of California, San Diego, and in History 264 at the State University of New York at Binghamton. Librarians at both institutions assisted students as they began to search for their own ethnic roots, and Paul Zarins, Susannah Galloway, and Ed Shephard have been particularly generous with their knowledge and time. The special collections departments at both libraries have graciously permitted students to deposit their papers in their collections, a fact that made this book possible. However effective these courses have been, graduate teaching assistants have made a major contribution, and in this regard I acknowledge the fine work of Art McEvoy, Victoria Brown, Scott Nash, Mike Groth, and Michelle Kuhl.

As the work of collecting papers for use in this volume proceeded it often required real detective work to track down former students and secure permission to use their writing. Mae Brown, Sonya Dublin, and Michelle Kuhl were instrumental in this phase of the work. Julie Simmonds and Laura Free provided additional typing, editing, and research assistance that helped bring the manuscript together. My thanks go out as well to Lois DeFleur and Sascha Dublin, who, hearing me talk at length about the wonder of these papers, insisted that they would make an excellent book and prodded me to launch the undertaking in the face of numerous other demands on my time. I am grateful to Janet Francendese and Steve Brier at Temple University Press, whose thoughtful comments helped me frame more clearly the students' work and who were willing to make a commitment to this project at an early stage. In addition, Victoria Brown, Constance Coiner, Donna Gabaccia, and Dorothee Schneider offered thoughtful readings of my introduction and selected student essays. Finally, my thanks go to Kitty Sklar for incisive editing and enthusiastic support in the final stages of this project.

It has been a joy to rediscover the fine work these students have done over the years and to help guide a small fraction of it to a broader audience. I gratefully acknowledge the permission of my former students to include their papers and family photographs in this collection. The Center for Lowell History, the Lowell Historical Society, and the Solvay Public Library have also granted permission for inclusion of photographs here. These papers show the power of multiculturalism in the classroom and demonstrate how students and faculty can learn in a setting that affords respect and encourages self-exploration.

Becoming American, Becoming Ethnic

Introduction

A spirited debate on college campuses in recent years has focused on the content of the undergraduate curriculum. Advocates of reform and defenders of current practice square off on a central question: Should we continue to focus general education requirements around classic works in the Western civilization tradition, or should we broaden that canon to include other cultures and traditions?

This book enters that debate by offering examples of student writing that demonstrate the compelling importance of multicultural identities in students' lives. Written as "Roots" papers for an undergraduate course on American immigration and ethnicity, principally by students in their first two years of college, these essays show that students can make a significant contribution to our understanding of fundamental social processes in American society in the late twentieth century.

The essays and poems in this book were written between 1977 and 1994 by students at two campuses of major state universities, the University of California, San Diego, and the State University of New York at Binghamton. The essays demonstrate that many of these students do not occupy a comfortable place in American society. They are sometimes excruciatingly aware of the cultural boundaries they must cross to succeed in their own cultural setting and in the larger dominant culture to which the university gives them access. At the university in general, and in this course in particular, they have struggled to understand this cultural process and its discontinuities and to come to terms with its meaning in their own lives and in the larger society.

These essays speak movingly about individual lives, but the fact that all were written by young people attending two state universities in the past twenty years also highlights the role of public higher education in the United States today. Public universities continue to offer immigrants and the children of immigrants the means for personal growth and development and the chance to explore "American" values even while they are in the midst of assessing their own inherited values. These essays reveal how vital this process is to the maintenance of democratic traditions in the United States, for despite their differences these students are all involved in the same fundamental activity: constructing an identity that is both personal and social, private and public. These essays should give pause to those in our society—particularly prominent in the states of California and New York—who are promoting regressive and short-sighted public policies that threaten to dismantle the systems of higher education that offer this opportunity for self-reflection and growth to talented members of less privileged groups.

Although from the start I appreciated the social significance of this student writing, I did not immediately act on this understanding. Over the years I had reproduced some of the papers for use in subsequent classes, and each year I asked a few students to read their papers to the class as a whole. Still, I felt strongly that the essays deserved an audience beyond this specific course; to friends and family I described the struggles these essays revealed and the richness of the perspectives they offered. Finally, others who responded to my enthusiasm about the work convinced me that I should edit a collection of the papers for publication.

As I assembled the collection I was gratified by the enthusiasm with which former students greeted the project. They were eager to see their work reach a broad audience and responded generously to editorial suggestions and requests for family photographs. Together we reached a shared understanding that theirs were more than personal stories, that their essays revealed how extremely diverse students at opposite sides of the country share common struggles in dealing with issues of identity in a multicultural society.

These essays, so expressive of the struggles of recent college students, should prove useful in a number of contexts. Teachers of writing know that students learn most effectively when their writing engages them personally. These essays offer particularly rich examples of engaged, first-person prose and of the value of linking personal experience with broader social processes. Written primarily by beginning college students, they offer examples of strong writing to their peers in introductory composition courses. Their rich views of multicultural America and contemporary issues of identity are also relevant to college students in introductory courses in sociology, anthropology, and psychology. Finally, these essays should prove useful in the study of ethnic history and ethnicity in American society today. Through these essays students can move from theoretical concepts to everyday realities and observe how broad social processes work themselves out in daily lives.

Revising U.S. Immigration History

During the years that I have taught about immigration and ethnicity in the United States, these essays have become increasingly diverse in tandem with the readings I have assigned to students. When I began teaching this course in January 1977, American immigration was treated by historians as an almost exclusively European phenomenon. The available historical writings were commonly organized in terms of "first" and "second" waves of immigration, a conceptualization of the field that assumes the overwhelming importance of European immigration. There were scattered writings about Chinese and Japanese immigration, but they were more focused on dominant, white attitudes toward Asians than on the actual experiences of Asian immigrants themselves. The years since I began teaching this course have seen both a dramatic growth in contemporary immigration and a reconceptualization of immigration as a worldwide, rather than simply a European, phenomenon. There is now an extensive bibliography that permits one to integrate Asian and Latin American immigration into the course. It has truly become a multicultural course over the past two decades.[1]

The shifting conceptualization of U.S. immigration history provides a framework for viewing the personal and familial accounts offered in this volume. Before 1970 U.S. immigration was typically examined in isolation, viewed as a unique phenomenon in world history. Immigrants whose experiences were studied were almost entirely of European origins, and the focus was commonly on the process of assimilation once the immigrant landed on American shores. This focus, narrow as it was, was nonetheless understandable given the legal framework within which U.S. immigration occurred between 1924 and 1965. Immigration declined drastically after the passage of the Johnson-Reid Act in 1924, and the national origins quota system established by that legislation ensured that immigrants of European backgrounds would predominate among those granted admission thereafter. Within this new context it is not surprising that scholars focused their interpretive powers on the process of cultural assimilation that took on increased significance as immigration slowed.

The reopening of the gates to increased immigration with the repeal of national origins quotas in 1965 dramatically changed both the actuality of U.S. immigration and the way scholars conceptualized the phenomenon. Virginia Yans McLaughlin edited a collection of essays, *Immigration Reconsidered,* in which she summarized the ways that recent scholarship challenged the earlier "accepted wisdom." Three developments seemed particularly crucial from her vantage point: "the international ecology of migration; a questioning of the classical assimilation model . . . and . . . a denial of American exceptionalism."[2] She highlighted a new willingness to place American immigration within the worldwide movements of people that have accompanied the internationalization of industrial capitalism over the past two centuries. These movements have included internal migration within nations, migration within Europe and Asia, migration across the Pacific as well as the Atlantic, migration to Latin America and Australasia as well as to North America, and finally, return migration to emigrants' countries of origin.

American immigration remains an important element in this more broadly conceived phenomenon, but it is now viewed on a wider canvas and no longer appears unique. Within this new conceptual framework, the phenomenon of immigrant assimilation becomes only one among a great variety of cultural responses to the challenges posed by the economic and social changes entailed in migration.[3] Although my teaching typically focused more on the immigration experience than on historical interpretations of the phenomenon, student explorations of their own ethnicity reinforced the broadening of perspective evident in the writings of professional historians.

The shifting vantage point of the course no doubt reflected the changing nature of U.S. immigration and of writings about immigration in this period, but I also responded to the growing diversity of my students, a phenomenon evident at both universities at which I taught. When I began teaching at the University of California, San Diego, about 15 percent of entering first-year students were black, Hispanic, or Asian American. By 1994 minority students comprised almost 30 percent of entering full-time students at the State University of New York at Binghamton.[4]

Memory, History, and Identity

The ethnic makeup of the students I have taught has evolved since I began teaching this course, but my approach to the "Roots" paper assignment has been consistent: I provided students with relatively flexible guidelines; I encouraged them to interview parents, grandparents, or other relatives and think about the changing meaning of ethnicity in their family; I asked them to reflect on the significance of ethnicity in their own lives and consider its meaning within the historical experience of their family. The assignment required them to think about their family within the broader context of immigration and ethnicity in the nation's history.[5] Lastly, I offered them the opportunity to deposit their papers in special collections in university archives for use by students and scholars.

These essays are typically the products of bright, beginning college students—predominantly students in their first two years of college who had come directly from high school. There were older, returning students and advanced undergraduates sprinkled through the class, but not many. Few had previously given much thought to the meaning of ethnicity in their lives, though those students who were African American, Hispanic, or Asian American were more conscious of their ethnicity than were those of white European descent.

These essays draw primarily on personal, familial sources and only occasionally on related scholarship. Not all the comparisons and contrasts drawn would withstand careful scrutiny; even the facts noted in placing a family's experience within a broader context are not always accurate. The writing, moving in many cases, can also be awkward at times. In editing these essays for publication, I have offered suggestions but have tried not to homogenize the writing or muffle the distinct "voices" that emerged. I sought to help the students communicate their ideas and experiences rather than produce polished prose. In all cases, students have had an opportunity to respond to editorial suggestions, have offered their own revisions, and have approved the publication of their essays.

As editor, I have generally accepted their revisions, except for cases in which the rewriting would have materially changed the original paper. It seemed important to preserve the integrity of the papers' content even when the older graduates today might be able to write more sophisticated or polished papers. These student "Roots" papers are rich examples of exercises in historical memory and the construction of identity rather than historical writing per se. Students brought to the assignment ideas and expectations that came from their own experiences. They commonly interviewed older family members who themselves offered another set of filters for the family's historical experience. We will probably never know if the stories they tell about themselves and their families are "true"—whether an exhaustive attempt to find corroborating contemporary evidence would bear out the versions of events presented here. Still, these stories have a meaning, a truth, to the students who wrote them. They have distilled from the stories they were told and from their own experiences the particular meanings these events had for them at the time they wrote these papers. As such, they provide rich source material for anyone interested in the meaning of ethnicity among college students in the past two decades.[6]

I began working on this collection by reading many of the student papers deposited in the libraries of the University of California, San Diego, and the State University of New York at Binghamton. I selected fifty or sixty essays from each university for further consideration. The numbers were purposely larger than I could include in this volume to allow for attrition as I contacted student authors and to permit me to make final selections in a way that took into account the themes of the essays and identities of their authors. Then I tried to reach all the student authors and secure their permission to consider the essays for publication. Ultimately I succeeded in reaching about sixty students, and it was from their work that I selected the essays published here. Given the time that had elapsed since I had taught in San Diego, I had more success in reaching former Binghamton students, a fact that accounts in part for the relative balance of the essays published here.

As I read over the essays and thought about which to include in the collection, they seemed to fall into three groupings. The largest group consisted of third-person accounts of the immigration or migration experiences of grandparents or more distant relatives. Students typically based these essays on interviews with their parents or other family members and reconstructed the experiences of one or two sets of grandparents. They also often addressed the changing significance of ethnicity with the passage of time between their grandparents' generation and their own. They viewed their attitudes toward their own ethnic identity as very much the product of a historical process that involved their grandparents, their parents, and themselves.

For the authors of the two remaining groups of essays the impact of immigration was more direct. One group of essays focused on the students' immigrant parents and the impact of their parents' ethnicity on their own lives. For these students, generational conflict lay at the center of their stories. Their lives revolved around the different experiences that they and their parents had in the United States and the conflict between the expectations of their parents and the pressure of their peers. The final set of essays are first-person accounts exploring issues of race and ethnicity in the lives of student authors who are themselves immigrants. Intergenerational conflicts are less pronounced for these students. Their concerns focus instead on issues of multiple and conflicting identities, and several students describe how they have vacillated between extremes at different points in their lives—at times identifying themselves as Americans, at other times as Mexican or Indian or whatever their particular nativity. The shifts in cultural identity that occurred across two, three, or four generations in the other essays are compressed within a single lifetime, often within a single decade, in these final accounts.

Most of the essays in this collection address the experiences of immigrants or the children and grandchildren of immigrants, and the accounts written by African Americans speak to many of the same issues. It is particularly striking in reading through the essays how often students of quite different racial and ethnic groups describe basically parallel cultural experiences. LaToya Powell begins her account on precisely this point: "Although generations before me did not come to the United States from a different country, we as African Americans have endured our own form of immigration." She goes on to describe the different ways that she and her migrant grandfather relate to dominant white culture in terms that reveal generational differences strikingly parallel to those for European-born immigrant grandparents and their U.S.-born grandchildren.

The essays offer countless examples of the shared cultural experiences of students from very different ethnic backgrounds. Thus students of Finnish (Tanya Mlodzinski), Korean (Sang-Hoon Kim), and Mexican (Jaime Dominguez) descent can each describe periods in their lives when they identified strongly as "Americans" and resented their parents' ethnic identification. All came over time to appreciate their ethnic background and to overcome an earlier need to distance themselves from those ethnic roots.

Similarly, students from different backgrounds can describe themselves as having multiple identities and see themselves as synthesizing the best features of several cultures. Shana Rivas sees Puerto Rican and African American culture as equally important in her identity; Melissa Algranati embraces her Egyptian Sephardic Jewish and Puerto Rican Catholic traditions; and Puwat Charukamnoetkanok acknowledges his triple identity, as Chinese, Thai, and American. For those of us who teach, our classes are multicultural not just because our students come from diverse backgrounds. As individuals many students themselves are multicultural because their families are blended by parentage across racial, ethnic, and national boundaries. This hybridity of our students has implications for our teaching. It is important for students to understand the varied experiences and cultures of different groups not simply to learn to respect and accommodate others, but also to understand themselves—and to understand the varied cultures that have contributed to their own identities.

These student essays show that the forging of a new national identity—a theme so much a part of the history of the United States—continues in the present. The French-born immigrant J. Hector St. John de Crèvecoeur posed the question in 1782, and Americans continue to answer it more than two hundred years later: "What then is the American, this new man?"[7] Although we rephrase this question in more gender-neutral terms today, Crèvecoeur's version and ours address the cultural consequences of the multi-ethnic nature of American society. The essays in this volume help us understand the construction of American identity in the late twentieth century, in fact, along much broader racial, ethnic, and national lines than in Crèvecoeur's lifetime. By entering into these accounts, we gain insights into the nature of American society today and into ourselves. Multiculturalism in the classroom and in American society throws new and useful light on longstanding and important questions. We come away from the encounter with understandings at once new and yet steeped in tradition.

Notes

1. This contrast emerges quite starkly in a comparison of the documentary collection I used when I first taught the course, Stanley Feldstein and Lawrence Costello, eds., *The Ordeal of Assimilation: A Documentary History of the White Working Class* (New York: Anchor Books, 1974) and the overview text I first used in 1995, Ronald Takaki, *A Different Mirror: A History of Multicultural America* (Boston: Little, Brown, 1993).

Two useful works that draw on this new bibliography are Roger Daniels, *Coming to America: A History of Immigration and Ethnicity in American Life* (New York: HarperCollins, 1990) and Alejandro Portes and Rubén Rumbaut, *Immigrant America: A Portrait* (Berkeley: University of California Press, 1990).

2. Virginia Yans McLaughlin, ed., *Immigration Reconsidered: History, Sociology, and Politics* (New York: Oxford University Press, 1990), 6.

3. For a similar discussion of the transformation of the study of European emigration in this same period, see the introduction to Rudolph J. Vecoli and Suzanne M. Sinke, eds., *A Century of European Migrations, 1830–1930* (Urbana: University of Illinois Press, 1991).

4. My thanks to Mae Brown at Thurgood Marshall College at the University of California, San Diego, and Geoffrey Gould, director of admissions, State University of New York at Binghamton, for the statistics offered here.

5. See the Appendix for a sample of the assignment to which students were responding in writing their papers.

6. For an excellent group of articles addressing the issues of historical memory and the construction of identity, see "Memory and American History," a special issue of *Journal of American History* 75 (March 1989). See also Michael Frisch, *A Shared Authority: Essays in the Craft and Meaning of Oral and Public History* (Albany: State University of New York Press, 1990); Ronald J. Grele, ed., *Envelopes of Sound: The Art of Oral History,* 2d ed. (New York: Praeger, 1991). In reflecting on these essays, I am aware of how much the perspectives I offered in course lectures and the questions I posed in the assignment helped shape student thinking about their own ethnic roots. As Frisch has emphasized in his explorations of oral history, my students and I have a "shared authority" in the portrait of contemporary ethnicity that emerges in this volume.

For a similar point about oral history evidence, see Studs Terkel, *Hard Times: An Oral History of the Great Depression* (New York: Avon, 1971), 17.

7. J. Hector St. John de Crèvecoeur, *Letters from an American Farmer and Sketches of Eighteenth-Century America* (1782; reprint, New York: Penguin, 1981), 70, as quoted in Arthur M. Schlesinger Jr., *The Disuniting of America,* (Knoxville, Tenn.: Whittle Direct Books, 1991), 1. I have quoted Crèvecoeur and addressed related themes in a more strictly historical context in the introduction to *Immigrant Voices: New Lives in America, 1773–1986* (Urbana: University of Illinois Press, 1993).

PART I

Family Traditions

The fourteen essays in this section explore family histories that begin with the immigration or migration experiences of great-grandparents and grandparents of the student authors. The essays are organized chronologically by the dates of migration of the central family members on whom the essays focus, ranging from the experience of an immigrant family from the Portuguese Azores in 1899 to that of an African American migrant from North Carolina to New York City in 1957.[1]

Broad patterns of immigration are reflected in the makeup of the immigrants described in these pages and in the nature of their experiences. Given the dates of immigration or migration—from 1899 to 1957—it should not be surprising that Europeans predominate in the accounts. Nonetheless, Puerto Rican, Mexican, and African American migrants appear toward the end of this time period.

Two contrasting themes recur in this section. Several of the stories offer glowing accounts of successful assimilation of family members over time, stressing economic success or, more commonly, the emergence of increasingly "Americanized" family members. In contrast, a somewhat larger number of authors stress the persistence of ethnic distinctiveness, generally expressing satisfaction in the way family members have maintained particularly strong bonds within their own ethnic group. Like broader American society itself, the authors make diverse judgments about the value of assimilation within mainstream American culture.

Several authors offer positive accounts of their families' assimilation into the dominant culture. Michele Kitko tells the story of her grandfather, who arrived with his parents at Ellis Island in 1908 and worked initially in Pennsylvania coal mines. Hers is the progressive story of immigrant assimilation and success across the generations. Stephanie Courtney relates her family's immigration experiences in similar terms, as "a shining example of the 'immigrant success story.'" Marc Turetzky and Rachel Koch each describe the increasing assimilation of their families across the generations, though as with the others, this assimilation is not inconsistent with a strong respect for earlier ethnic traditions.

In other essays, the persistence of ethnic distinctiveness is more striking than a progressive Americanization. Virginia Correia's discussion of her family's emigration from the Portuguese Azores is a case in point. Beginning with her great-grandfather, all of Virginia's forebears found marriage partners from among fellow immigrants from Terceira in the Azores. The continuous infusion of new Terceiran immigrants into the Gonsalves-Pine-Correia family reinforced the Portuguese cultural heritage that might otherwise have been diluted.

Other authors describe patterns of their families' persistent ethnicity in similar terms. Raffi Ishkanian traces the role of his family's Armenian cultural traditions in the lives of his grandparents and parents, and acknowledges the importance of those traditions in his own life. Josephine Burgos rejects a stereotypically negative view of the Puerto Rican homeland of her parents and grandparents as she affirms the continuing cultural significance of the island in her own life.

In the end there is no single "typical" relationship between the authors of these essays and the ethnic traditions of their forebears. We might better view these relationships as a continuum. At one extreme are those students who view themselves as "American" or as a blend of a variety of ethnic traditions. At the other extreme are those who see themselves as distinctively ethnic and proud of that heritage. In between, we find others who accept some of the values and traditions of their grandparents and yet acknowledge the significant cultural differences that have emerged over time.

Note

1. To help in identifying the papers, the date of the paper and the university where the paper was written (University of California, San Diego, or State University of New York at Binghamton) follow the author's name. Further information about the papers' authors is given in the Notes on Contributors.

Virginia Correia (UC San Diego 1984)

Life after Terceira

The process of Portuguese immigration in my family's history extends back to the beginning of the twentieth century. As you read this essay, you will see how the process of assimilation has affected the first immigrants in my family, beginning with my great-grandfather and great-grandmother and ending with my father and brother-in-law. You will also be able to see the common process of immigration that runs through their experiences, including the types of jobs immigrants first held and a common first place of residence—Lowell, Massachusetts.

In the year 1899 a nine-year-old boy by the name of Louis F. Gonsalves arrived in Boston. He emigrated with his family from the island of Terceira, located off the coast of Portugal and belonging to a chain of islands known as the Azores. Louis and his family made their permanent residence in the city of Lowell, Massachusetts. Louis was able to adapt well to the American way of life. He learned to speak English by attending public schools until the age of twelve. At that time, he journeyed to California and became a shepherd. He stayed in California for five years. Upon returning to Lowell, he met and married Guilhermina N. Borges.

Guilhermina was also born on the island of Terceira. She immigrated to the United States in 1902 at the age of fifteen. Her father worked in the textile mills of Lowell. Guilhermina was a weaver employed by Appleton Mills in Lowell. Guilhermina did not adapt well to her new society. She remained mainly among Portuguese-speaking people and never really learned to speak the English language. She married Louis F. Gonsalves, and they had five children: Mary, Virginia, Edward, Ida, and John.

Group photo at Appleton Mills, Lowell, Massachusetts, 1913. Guilhermina Borges was a weaver and is seated in the front row just behind the right elbow of the standing male overseer. Her sister, who worked in the mill with her, is on the other side of the overseer. (Courtesy Lowell Historical Society)

Virginia Correia's great-grandparents, Louis and Guilhermina Gonsalves, with their first child, Mary.

The family moved to many different locations in California until they settled in Pico. Louis worked at several odd jobs until he was finally able to make his living as a dairy farmer. He was the sole support of the family except for several boarders who paid for their keep by working in the dairy.

Virginia Gonsalves, the second-born daughter of Louis and Guilhermina, and my grandmother, worked with her father and mother by helping with the chores of bookkeeping, feeding boarders, and other endless household duties. Virginia was also the first in the family to complete high school. At the age of seventeen, she met Joseph C. Pine. After going through a semisecret courtship, because of her father's unwillingness to accept Joseph into the family, Virginia married Joseph at the age of nineteen; he was twenty-eight.

Joseph C. Pine was born in Providence, Rhode Island, in 1909. When he was an infant, his parents went back to their native homeland of Terceira, Azores. Joseph remained in the Azores until the age of eighteen when he came back to the United States and made his home in California. He worked as a dairy milker all his life. At the age of twenty-six, while employed by Louis Gonsalves, he met Virginia, and they were later married. The couple worked together trying to establish their own dairy business before and after the depression years, and became successful in their venture. Their average income in 1937 was ninety dollars per month.

Joe and Virginia had four children, and all but one died of childhood diseases. The only surviving child, Eva Joyce Pine, is my mother. Eva was born in Hanford, California, but was raised on her parents' new dairy located in Artesia, California. In the year 1960, at the age of sixteen, Eva met Joseph C. Correia—a Portuguese immigrant from Terceira who had just arrived in the United States through the port of New York. Joseph adapted readily to his new life in the United States. He had friends, relatives, and a job waiting for him on the California coast.

Joseph and Eva went through a lengthy courtship of two years. They were unable to date through their entire engagement, and their only visits had to be done through the screen door of her home. They married in 1962, and Joseph went to work for Eva's father, Joseph Pine, in the dairy. During their marriage, Joseph insisted that Eva teach him the English language because he did not want any of his children to have to struggle because of the inability to speak English.

Joseph and Eva had three children: Annette Marie, Virginia Ann, and Joseph Pine. All three children were raised in the dairy and rural atmosphere with Portuguese traditions.

The eldest of the children, Annette, married her third cousin, who is also an immigrant from the island of Terceira. His name is Manuel Braulio Machado. Manuel migrated with his family to Montreal. Manuel assimilated perfectly into the Canadian atmosphere. He learned to speak French and English, but he did not lose the use of his own native language. Manuel and Annette met at the ages of fifteen and thirteen, respectively, when Manuel came with his family to see my grandparents, Joseph and Virginia. Annette and Manuel corresponded for seven years until he moved with his family to Tulare, California, in April 1983. In November 1983, Manuel and Annette were married.

Throughout every generation, all the women in my family (except for me) have been married to emigrants from Terceira, Azores. Through marriage they have reinforced the link to their Portuguese blood. They have all found a way of holding onto their heritage. I feel as if I have lost touch with mine. As bilingual educators have noted, "children lose a degree of 'individuality' by becoming assimilated into public society."[2] I feel I have lost part of my individuality by not being able to share my Portuguese heritage with my parents because they wanted me to be an "American."

My parents taught me well—too well, in fact. I became more American than they realized and lost my individuality by completely accepting a new culture and assimilating. The choice to leave for college was very difficult and it further alienated me from my Portuguese heritage. My sister lived up to my family's expectations perfectly, and my brother expressed no desire to go to college or leave home. My experience has been different and I am looked at as rebellious and defiant. I left home and left my Portuguese roots behind.

Note

1. As quoted in Richard Rodriguez, *Hunger of Memory: The Education of Richard Rodriguez* (Boston: David R. Godine, 1981), 26. Rodriguez critiques this idea, but it is consistent with my own experience.

Tanya Mlodzinski (SUNY Binghamton 1989)

Coming to Terms with My Heritage

Growing up in Yonkers, New York, during the 1950s and 1960s, I had always scorned my Finnish heritage because it was so different within that environment. I remember being the subject of much teasing due to my "funny" name—Tanya Kaartinen—and the even more peculiar ones of my parents—Toini and Onni. Many of my peers had never heard of Finland. Yet a few elementary school projects elicited some pride in my nationality; my parents were very education minded and it was a way to impress my teachers. Our Yonkers neighborhood was largely one of Italians and Poles; my mother and father never truly assimilated there—until recently, 95 percent of the people with whom they associated were Finnish. In fact, the only reason they settled in that city shortly after World War II was because my father was asked to join the editorial staff of a Finnish newspaper there.

My parents were excited at the prospect of this essay because in the last few years, after their first trip to Finland, they have attempted some worthwhile research into their own family histories. Sadly, until now, I have not shown much interest in their findings. Additionally, I have given my own three children virtually no impetus for interest in their Finnish heritage. We practice no Finnish customs, attend no Finnish activities (though they are prevalent in the Finger Lakes area), and have no Finnish friends. My sisters and I each married non-Finns and, as far as I know, their relation of family history to their children and their ethnic practices are minimal. I guess this stems from the fact that we have always been slightly perturbed by our parents' apparent inclination toward exclusive Finnish associations. Everything they have done has had ethnic influence. It is my observation that this is true for all the Finns of their generation, and the observation of historians that it was also true of those before them: "As soon as they came to America, Finnish immigrants sought each other's companionship. . . . Next they developed their companionship into formal organizations. . . . Then with messianic fervor they endorsed mental improvement and proclaimed that organized minds were power. By seeking mastery of their own minds through the organizations, the immigrants finally found their America and intellectual independence from Finland."[1]

Both my parents, in their histories, have related organizational activities and ethnic "enclavity." Eloise Engle attributes this to *sisu,* which means "something like solid—even stolid—obstinance [*sic*], patience, bull-headedness, guts."[2] I add tenacity. My forebears have certainly exhibited these characteristics.

Each set of grandparents was part of the exodus of the 360,000 Finns who immigrated to North America between 1864 and 1920, incorporated within the "new wave" of immigration from Eastern and Southern Europe.[3] Alfred Kaartinen, son of Finnish peasants, came to Ironwood, Michigan, in 1903. His future wife, Lili Herlevi, came at approximately the same time, apparently alone, to Minneapolis. Why they came is unclear, though economic betterment is most likely; Alfred was the eldest of twelve children in a poor family. Married in Ironwood in 1906, they operated a small restaurant for a time, in addition to his work in the mines there. The first two of eight children were born there, my father in 1910. In 1911 the family moved to a tract of land in a railroad stop—DeFer, Wisconsin, about six miles from Hurley. Here they attempted small farming and various kinds of industry. According to my father, Alfred tried to "keep up with the times." He experimented with new crops, was the first in the area to buy a car, and installed carbide lighting in their home; he also promoted joint projects for the purchase of modern farm machinery. Because the farm did not prosper, despite his efforts, he also conducted rentals and purchases, singly or with neighbors, of stands of timber to be felled and sold to sawmills. He also managed a cooperative store and cooperative creamery at different times. The idea of cooperatives was important to Finns for economic reasons, but also because it allowed them to shop in places they could call their own and where they could conduct business in Finnish. By 1916 there were about seventy Finnish co-ops in the United States.[4]

Though their first farm community was entirely Finnish, both quickly became U.S. citizens and acquired command of the English language. In DeFer, both served as postmaster. Alfred occasionally served as interpreter at judicial proceedings, was chairman of the town board, and sought nomination for the state assembly on the Progressive Party ticket. Later he helped form the Farm-Labor Party in Wisconsin. He was also a frequent speaker at Finnish gatherings and a contributor to Finnish newspapers. Social life included visits to neighbors for work bees, coffee, games, and participation in the all-important sauna, for every rural Finn home had one. (My father later built one in the basement of our Yonkers home.) There were also frequent visits to the local Finnish Farmers Club. In town, my father belonged to a larger Finnish club, part of a youth group and calisthenics group, which also engaged in much singing, dancing, and acting. His first school consisted entirely of Finnish students; however, the teachers were non-Finns and roomed with local families, including my father's. He and a schoolmate were the first to attend high school from their small rural community. Severe illness delayed his enrollment (he was thought to be tubercular) and prevented high school track and field activities, which he loved.

It seems that it was during these years and a subsequent brief work experience in Chicago that my father had his first major contact with non-Finns. He did well in school and had planned to enter the University of Wisconsin. When his father became ill, however, work was essential, so he traveled to Chicago and was employed by a brokerage firm through the events of the 1929 Crash. As a result of activities in the Chicago Finnish Club, part of a national organization, he became district organizer, to help recruit new members—American-born Finns—since current members were aging and new immigration had been restricted. This participation improved his Finnish, which had deteriorated in school, and in 1935, he was invited to join the editorial staff of a Finnish newspaper in Superior, Wisconsin. Soon after, he volunteered to support the popular government in Spain against Franco, but the national Finnish leadership intervened; they wanted him to become the secretary of the Finnish Workers Federation. This involved a move to New York City and, in his own words, more involvement in Finnish activities with extensive traveling, speaking, and lecturing. It was on one such speaking engagement in Spencer, New York, that he met my mother, Toini Mattinen. They were married in 1940.

Even during wartime service in Australia, my father sought Finnish servicemen and families through telephone directories and the classification department, where he worked. Had my parents moved to Superior from

Työmies Eteenpäin

FINNISH NATION-WIDE WEEKLY — SUPERIOR, WISCONSIN

NO. 20 — TORSTAINA, 25. TOUKOKUUTA 1989 — THURSDAY, MAY 25, 1989 — 87. vuosikerta — VOLUME 40

Gorba lähti Kiinasta, mellakat jatkuvat

BEJING, Kiina — Jo viikko sitten Kiinasta kotiutunut Neuvostoliiton puoluejohtaja ja preseidentti Mihail Gorbatshov pitäytyi tyystin erillään Kiina sisäisestä tilanteesta, mutta korosti matkansa tärkeyttä maiden välisille suhteille. — Olihan Neuvostoliiton johtaja vierailulla Kiinassa ensi kerran 30:een vuoteen.

Vierailusta annetussa tiedonannossa todettiin, että huipputapaaminen merkitsee valtioiden välisten suhteiden normalisoitumista, mitä ei kuitenkaan ole tähdätty kolmansia maita vastaan.

Uutistoimisto Tassin raportissa todettiin Kiinan opiskelijamellakoiden laajentuneen työläisten keskuuteen. Kiinalaiset vaativat enemmän poliittista vapautta ja lahjonnan lopettamista.

Taivaallisen rauhan aukiolla jo toista viikkoa jatkunut mielenosoitus on

Opiskelijamielenosoitukset Beijingissä jatkuivat opiskelijoiden ja hallituksen neuvotteluiden katkettua heti alkuunsa.

tyivät heti alkuunsa, koska pääministeri ei myöntynyt neuvotteluiden suoraan televisiointiin. Tassin mukaan Beijingin suurimpien tehtaiden työläiset ja valtion virastojen virkailijat ovat

opiskelijoille: "Me viisi miljoonaa valtiontilojen työntekijää tuemme teitä", tai "Pelastakaa opiskelijat". Mielenosoittajat lauloivat "Kansainvälistä".

Toistaiseksi Kiinan mielenosoituk-

Suomesta 150 nuoriso-festivaaleille

Suomesta lähtee maailman nuorten ja opiskelijoiden 13. festivaaleille Korean demokraattiseen tasavaltaan 150 nuorta. Heinäkuun alussa järjestettäviin festivaaleihin osallistuvat nuoret edustavat suomalaisia opiskelija- ja nuorisojärjestöjä laidasta laitaan.

Front page from the Finnish national daily *Työmies Eteenpäin* (Workingman Forward), Superior, Wisconsin, 25 May 1989. From 1935 to 1937 Onni Kaartinen, Tanya Mlodzinski's father, worked for *Työmies* in Superior, Wisconsin. After World War II he worked for *Eteenpäin* in Yonkers. In 1951 the two newspapers merged and were thereafter published in Superior.

Yonkers, after the war, when the Finnish newspaper did, my Finnish associations would have been much more viable.

I had always thought that I was of "pure" Finnish descent; however, my mother's maternal great-great-grandparents were both Swedish. Their son Henrik married a Sophia Holm, of German descent. Their daughter Sannaliisa married Kalle Muurinaho, whose oldest daughter, Hilja, is my grandmother. Kalle, like my mother's father, had made several trips to North America before bringing his family to Canada—working in the lumber industries of Florida, the Midwest, and Washington. It was unusual that they came at all, for they were large landowners in Finland.

My mother was born in Sudbury, Ontario, Canada, of immigrants from Vaasa, which along with the province of Oulu, provided 60 percent of Finnish emigrants.[5] Her paternal grandparents were also large landholders. It is unclear why her father left; as the third son of ten children, he was offered the farm when his father died—his two older brothers having already acquired divisions. He, however, had been to Canada, in the 1890s, and wanted to return. Just after the turn of the century, he emigrated to Mond, Ontario, married, had two children, and worked in the booming nickel mines there. When his wife contracted tuberculosis, she wanted to return to Finland to be "cured"—she died aboard ship and was buried in Liverpool, England. A widower with two young children, Jacob continued on to Finland where his infant son died soon thereafter. He remarried there—to Hilja—and before long left again for Canada, later to send tickets to his wife, sister, and daughter. In Mond, they took over management of a large boarding house—*poikatalot*—typical of Finnish communities consisting of many young men. My grandmother was just nineteen. There was much correspondence with family in Finland, and a few of her younger sisters later joined them. (I have a large number of maternal relatives still living in the Sudbury/Mond area.) Finnish cultural activities abounded in their community—halls with dances, plays, choruses, and sporting events. "Finn Halls" became landmarks wherever Finns settled, and political organizations, gymnastic societies, fraternal orders, and mixed choruses were an integral part of Finnish groupings.[6] I have been to many such halls in my lifetime, often performing myself.

The flu epidemic of 1918, the year of my mother's birth, hit hard (my grandfather carted bodies for burial), and the Mond mine closed soon afterward. The family immigrated to the United States and purchased a rundown farm in Rudyard, Michigan. Finances were difficult, so Jacob worked in the lumber camps prevalent in the area, coming home every week or so. In the early 1920s, hearing of mining jobs in New Jersey, they

Wedding portrait, 1910, Hilja and Jacob Mattinen. The couple courted in Finland. Jacob immigrated to Canada, then sent a ticket for Hilja. They married in Sudbury, Ontario, where the photo was taken. Hilja and Jacob were Tanya Mlodzinski's grandparents.

Hilja and Jacob Mattinen's boardinghouse, Mond, Ontario, 1910. Hilja is seated in the back row with a baby in her lap. Jacob is barely visible in the window behind his wife.

moved again, to Richard Mines. Twice more before my mother started school, they moved to where there were jobs—to Scrub Oaks, New Jersey, and to Coleville, Pennsylvania. Prior to 1926 they moved twice more, to Bellefonte and Wilkes-Barre, Pennsylvania, where anthracite mining was at its peak. They lived in Finnish communities of various sizes; my grandmother never learned to speak English. With the stock market crash, the Mattinens decided to buy a farm in order to become more self-sufficient, and thus moved to the Finnish community of Van Etten, New York, near where I now live. This was a beautiful hundred-acre farm with a lovely house. Jacob commuted to Wilkes-Barre for a while; Hilja and the children were in charge of the farm. My mother claims that with the help of an enterprising Finnish real estate agent, the Spencer–Van Etten–Newfield area was bought up by Finns in the early 1900s. They purchased dilapidated farms that the "Yankees" had abandoned and turned them into productive dairy and poultry farms. Of course, there was the all-important Spencer Co-op Society, run by Finns, which provided many jobs and eventually became a $1 million business.

Their lovely farm burned in the 1930s and they moved to another, smaller, place in Spencer. Jacob succumbed to the mine disease, anthrasilicosis, or "black lung"; Hilja married Matti Wick (who had held the secretary's position my father gained) and stayed on that farm. My father's parents also came to Spencer, to a farm bought for them by my parents soon after their marriage. These are the places of my fond childhood memories; through frequent visits I have witnessed the decay of the grand farms and the demise of the thriving Finnish community. When my husband and I decided to move out of Yonkers, I encouraged settlement in this area of my relatives—my living roots. My parents soon followed. It is in these memories that I sense a retention of ethnic awareness, that, while not active, is a comforting part of my life. There is an indescribable feeling that comes with reading names and dates relating to me—to know that these were real people, with real struggles. Ours pale by comparison.

I cannot blame my parents for their strict ethnic affiliations. It was typical of other groups as well. We were always included, and we had fun. Opening presents on Christmas Eve, in the Finn custom, was wonderful, and Finnish pulla is the best sweet bread in the world. Our trips to Saari Camps, in Massachusetts, the Midwest, and Canada were great vacations; our friends and relatives had the most beautiful lake cabins and interesting farms. Everything was Finn-related, but I have not suffered for it and have no doubt gained much from it. My parents have a wide circle of friends across the country and are well traveled and extremely active in their seventies. With their past few years' interest in square dancing, they've expanded their friendships to include all nationalities. They never discouraged association with other groups; it was just not part of their lives to encourage such. They both retain the Finnish language and are still active in Finnish "doings." It seems silly to have once been embarrassed by my heritage; I am now pleased to be part of a relatively small but vital group. My attendance at SUNY-Binghamton as an adult, full-time student gives me the courage to think that I retain that concept of *sisu*.

Notes

1. Arthur William Hoglund, *Finnish Immigrants in America, 1880–1920* (Madison: University of Wisconsin Press, 1960), 37.
2. Eloise Engle, *Finns in North America,* (Annapolis: Leeward Publications, 1975), 6.
3. Ibid., 28.
4. Ibid., 60.
5. Hoglund, *Finnish Immigrants in America,* 7.
6. Engle, *Finns in North America,* 52.

Sara Kindler (SUNY Binghamton 1992)

The Family History of a Fourth-Generation Pole

The Saturday before Easter 1992, my family and I traveled to Massachusetts to visit my grandmother for the holiday. I was able to interview her before the rest of our relatives arrived to partake of Granny's annual Easter borscht. That afternoon she helped me trace my maternal roots. I was really impressed by all the stories I had never heard before about my family's rich history.

In 1889 Antonina Rzeszutko, my maternal great-grandmother, was born in Wola-Lubecka, a small town in Poland. At the age of sixteen she traveled by boat, across the Atlantic, and reached Ellis Island. This young woman decided to leave her family and country behind, like many others at this time, due to her economic status in Poland and the promise of a better life in America, which she eventually found.

In the town where my great-grandmother lived (located in the southeasternmost corner of Poland) the economy was based on agriculture, and she lived on a small farm with her family. After 1864 and until the early 1900s, Poland experienced serious agricultural problems due to competition from Russia, America, and Australia.[1] The large landowners were able to handle these hard times better than the smaller landholders because they had the resources to industrialize. "*The small landowners* and peasants . . . could not avail themselves of the advantages afforded by the industrialization of agriculture. This fact clearly shows prejudice caused to them by the lack of technical education, of agricultural syndicates and of credit organizations."[2] The small-scale farmer was being shut out of the economy. The population of Poland was increasing at a tremendous rate in the second half of the nineteenth century, and the land could not support all of its people. Between 1890 and 1910 the population increased by 3.5 million.[3] Great emigration ensued for a period of twenty years. Several hundred thousand Poles left the country at this time to seek a better life.

My great-grandmother, Busia, as she is referred to in my family (it is the Polish word for grandmother), lived in a one-room house with her mother and father (Magdelena and Szezepan Rzeszutko) and her six sisters. In the winter when snows were shoulder high, it was impossible to go out and feed the two horses and milk the three cows, so then those animals stayed in the house with the family. A man from Busia's area offered to take her to America. The plan was that she would pose as his daughter. Busia jumped at this great opportunity and agreed to go. She desired a job, money, and a more comfortable life in the United States.

In 1906 Busia arrived at Ellis Island and then traveled to Utica, New York, where the man who brought her over had relatives and where Busia had a half-sister who barely knew her. Busia had been working in a cotton mill in Utica for a very short time when she was invited to a christening in Worcester, Massachusetts. Busia liked Worcester so much that she never went back to Utica. She sent for her belongings and moved to Massachusetts. It is amazing how much Busia went through at such a young age and in such a short period of time. She was very independent and brave. During our interview my grandmother referred to Busia as "spunky." I cannot think of a better word.

Busia moved to Webster, Massachusetts. What attracted her to this new locality was a large Polish community and a Polish Catholic church. There were many other nationalities in the community such as the Irish, French, and the Germans. These groups had their own churches with masses spoken in their own tongue by a fellow countryman. There were some streets where only Poles lived, or only Irish lived, but there were no ghettos of one group or another. Most streets had an intermingling of every ethnic group in the area. The various individuals from different nationalities were not completely isolated within their own groups; they interacted with each other and grew tolerant of the differences around them.

Busia was able to find work in Samuel Slater's cotton mill in the spinning room. Slater started the town of Webster with his mill in the early nineteenth century. There were many Polish women who worked there, and if it became necessary to communicate with the bosses, there usually was a girl who knew English and would act as an interpreter.

The Rzeszutko family homestead in southeastern Poland in Wola-Lubecka, in the province of Galicia. Photo taken in 1978.

The bed in which Busia slept when she was single was shared by two other girls. Busia was so happy when one of the girls got married because then she had more room in bed.

In 1909 Busia married John Ruda. Together they had seven children: Winifred, Rose (my grandmother, born in 1913), Stasia, John, Mary, Helen, and a first child who died very young. When the two first met, he worked as a weaver in the same mill as she did. She was nineteen and he was twenty-one. My family refers to him as Dziadzia, meaning grandfather. Dziadzia came to America also looking for a better life. What is interesting is that he and Busia had come from the same area in Poland, Galicia, but they first met in the United States.

The couple worked forty-eight hours a week at Slater's mill, including Saturdays. Both worked very hard because money was extremely important; they had to build new lives in this country. They were great savers because they had been so poor back in Poland. The first two weeks Dziadzia had been working at the mill he received no wages because the workers got paid every two weeks. He had no money and was too proud to ask for food, so when it got dark out he felt for cucumbers to eat in a nearby garden.

Until 1929 the Rudas lived in mill housing on Slater Street in Webster. When they first moved in, the rent was one dollar per week. Busia found an envelope with an old bill in it that said the rent for the previous occupants had been only eighty-five cents a week. The Rudas would not stand for being taken advantage of by the mill owners and brought their case to the company's attention. Thereafter they only had to pay the fair price of eighty-five cents a week.

Busia and Dziadzia kept in touch with their relatives back in Poland by mail. Busia often sent money to her parents. After she and Dziadzia were married and had saved up enough money, Busia was able to pay for the passage of one of her sisters, and Dziadzia did the same for his sister. The voyage cost one hundred dollars apiece. Their two sisters and another woman boarded with the Rudas for a while until they were settled in the new country. Later on, Busia's sister Catherine came over with her husband. They preferred Poland to America—"the air was better there"—and they moved back.

Discontented with mill work, Dziadzia bought a house with a dairy in June 1929, on the eve of the depression. The man who built this house had gone bankrupt. Dziadzia became a private businessmen and would often lend large sums of money to other Poles in the neighborhood who needed his help. He always trusted that they would return the money, and

Studio portrait, Webster, Massachusetts, ca. 1913. The woman on the left is Sara Kindler's great-grandmother, Busia (Antonina Rzeszutko). The child is Winifred, one of Sara's great-aunts.

they did. The dairy business introduced Dziadzia to many people of other ethnic origins because he sold his wares to all kinds of people, not just Poles. Polish was spoken in their home, but the Rudas picked up English gradually.

The language barrier did prove to be a problem in 1929 when Dziadzia needed a license to drive a truck for the dairy business. He could not read English so he had his daughter Rose get a license first because she could read English. Rose ended up helping her father to get his license by telling the Ford dealer in town that Dziadzia would buy a truck from him if he was able to get a license. Dziadzia took his driving tests, and he did everything wrong but passed anyway. The Ford dealer had paid off the inspector.

Coming from Polish parents in Webster, Massachusetts, had a great impact on my grandmother when she was growing up. Because Polish was spoken in the home when she was very young, sometimes it was hard for my grandmother to communicate with others in town. One day, Busia sent her to the store to buy some tea, but my grandmother could not say it in English. The storekeeper told her to point it out, but she could not and went home crying. Her sister could spell it and went back later to buy the tea.

The Rudas were able to get along well without learning English for a long time because there were so many other Poles living around them. The Polish Catholic Church was the center of their lives and the lives of the whole Polish community in Webster as well. It was extremely important. Many men donated a lot of money to the church and would work free for the church's needs. The church was a great unifying factor in the Polish community. "For most Poles until the nineteen forties and for many well after World War II, the parish-centered community provided the arena within which identity and status were worked out and most satisfactions and rewards were obtained."[4] Because of the great respect Poles had for the Catholic church, many Polish boys and girls became priests and nuns. My grandmother's sister Winifred became a nun.

After the third grade my grandmother went to Polish school, which was adjacent to the church. Twenty-three Polish nuns taught the children in both Polish and English. Religion was taught every day. The nuns said that it was a sin to go to a Protestant church. Once my grandmother went into the basement of a Protestant church and felt she had committed a horrible sin.

My grandmother was very much involved with her Polish heritage and community. She associated mostly with Polish people but was not isolated in this community by any means. She had friends of many different nationalities on her block. Also important was the fact that through some

John and Antonina Ruda and their six children in the early 1920s. Sara Kindler's grandmother, Rose Ruda, is standing at her mother's right shoulder.

public schooling and the teaching of English in the Polish school, she was able to learn English and therefore communicate with the non-Polish community.

My grandmother felt pressure from her parents and the rest of the Polish community to date only Polish men. My grandmother did not really mind because she knew she would marry a Polish man, but she wanted to have fun and did not limit herself to dating only Polish men. The one thing that was more important to my grandmother about her boyfriends than their ethnicity was their religion. Once she was dating a Russian and found out he went to a Russian church, so she stopped going out with him. My grandmother married Frank Wieloch, who was a Polish Catholic like herself.

Busia and Dziadzia did not forget their roots in Poland. In 1939 Dziadzia traveled there, but he had picked a bad time. On September first, Hitler bombed Warsaw, and Dziadzia was scared that he would never make it home to America. He eventually made his way back safely through Italy, but he was sorry he had visited Poland because it was in such a sorry state.

Busia went to her hometown in Poland in 1960 to visit her sisters; her mother had died in 1944. Everyone in Poland was so poor after the war, and she, too, was sorry she had visited. Busia asked her sisters where the beautiful dresses were that she had sent to them. Four were hanging in the closet because the women were saving them for their funerals. Busia did not understand why they did not want to look nice while they were living and wear their old dresses when they were dead. Busia had become very accustomed to her new American way of life. When she got back she was happy to be home in a nice hot bath.

Contact with Poland did not end with my great-grandparents. My grandmother helped bring Dziadzia's grandnephew, Adam Sujak, to this country. She and my grandfather Frank Wieloch lent him money and housed him until he could make a start for himself in Massachusetts. I remember the day Adam Sujak came to the country. He stayed at my family's house in New York for one night because he had just flown in that day. I saw part of a world that was very removed from me. Adam did not know any English, and my father, sister, and I knew no Polish. My mother could understand only a little Polish. My grandparents, however, spoke fluently with this foreigner. It was strange to think this man, who I could not even communicate with, was somehow related to me. It was quite an interesting experience.

I think my family survived so well in Webster because of the community they lived in and their own attitude toward that community. The town of Webster was made up of many different ethnic groups, and no one group was considered a minority, or different, because everyone was essentially different. The Polish community helped the Rudas to feel comfortable in the town as a whole. Prejudices existed between the various ethnic groups, but my ancestors did not want to hurt other people just because of their ethnicity, so they did well in society. For instance, my grandfather Frank Wieloch used to walk a fair distance to work every day because he could not leave the team of horses in town. A Frenchman, Mr. Durkee, would pass him in a team everyday, but would not offer my grandfather a ride because he was Polish. One day Durkee needed a ladder to paint his house and sent his sons to borrow one from my grandfather. My great-grandfather Dominic Wieloch told my grandfather not to lend them the ladder, but he did not listen and let them borrow it anyway. After that, Durkee would give my grandfather a ride to work.

I am very proud of my Polish heritage. I have great respect for my great-grandparents' ability to succeed in a new and foreign country. They created a healthy and happy atmosphere for their children. I also admire my grandparents for embracing their heritage and accepting different ethnic groups around them. I have enjoyed going to visit my grandparents in Massachusetts to eat Polish food, hear them speak Polish to their friends, and sometimes to attend their Polish church. It is nice to feel a sense of tradition, to feel part of the Polish people, and to feel part of their history, my history.

Notes

1. *The Polish Encyclopedia,* vol, 3, *Economic Life of Poland,* (1922; reprint, New York: Arno Press, 1972), 48, 396.
2. Ibid., 397.
3. Thaddeus C. Radzialowski, "The Polish American Experience," in *American Ethnic Profiles: Background Papers,* ed. Anthony Codianni (St. Paul: Immigration History Research Center, University of Minnesota, 1978), 35.
4. Ibid., 36.

Michele Kitko (UC San Diego 1982)

My Paternal Forebears

My paternal forebears left Austria-Hungary as a result of discontent with the monarchy and as a means toward realizing a value that in their lives had priority above all others. They sought in America a place where they and future generations could have a better life. The desire to better the lives of their children was so important to them that they willingly left their homeland and its people. Austria-Hungary failed to provide the opportunity they needed to better their lives—specifically, to own land—and so they voluntarily immigrated to America, a country that could provide the opportunity they sought. In order to utilize the opportunity that existed in America, they assimilated for the most part, although not entirely, into the American way of life. In their hearts was a dream; within their reach, a place that could fulfill this dream. My forebears became part of the place that made this dream possible and in becoming a part of it, their dream became a reality.

Life in the dual monarchy of Austria-Hungary during the 1890s was one of economic hardship. In a Slovakian region one hundred miles east of Bratislava, my paternal grandfather's family was suffering economically, as was the rest of the agrarian class of this period. My great-grandfather Joseph Kitko disliked Austria-Hungary and did not permit his children to attend Hungarian schools; thus my grandfather received no formal education during his childhood. Greater though, was my great-grandfather's discontent with the lack of opportunity in Austria-Hungary to better his life and the lives of his children. Because he placed such a high value on providing a better life for his family, he was willing to immigrate to America alone, to a country he believed would provide the opportunity that Austria-Hungary could not. The pull to America, a land of opportunity and a place to realize his dream, was greater than the push from Austria-Hungary where his life was beset with economic hardship and political discontent.

My grandfather Steven Paul Kitko, at the age of sixteen, along with his mother, brothers, and sister, crossed the Atlantic crowded in steerage on his way to America. The family arrived at Ellis Island in April 1908 and joined my great-grandfather and other relatives in the Slavic-populated coal mining town of Madera, Pennsylvania. Here, the family retained many of their old customs and spoke chiefly Slovak. Life was hard; the streets were not paved with gold as some stories went, but here existed the opportunity they sought—to better their lives.

In 1913, five years after my grandfather's arrival in America, he married my grandmother, Susanna Stroka—then fifteen years old—in what was more or less an arranged marriage. Her parents and older sisters had emigrated from the same region of Austria-Hungary for the same reason my grandfather had—to better their lives and the lives of their children. The family was, according to my grandmother, very happy in America and fit into the American way of life. My grandmother attended school through the third grade but quit because it was not required that she attend. Her family also lived in a region of Pennsylvania populated by Slavs, spoke little English, and retained many of their ties with Austria-Hungary. The retention of religious ties was shared by both families. My grandmother's and grandfather's families were Catholic and attended church regularly.

While both families preserved old customs during their years in Pennsylvania, they also assimilated into the American lifestyle. They had voluntarily left Austria-Hungary to seek a home in America. Whatever it took to become American, they were willing to do. Living among their countrymen resulted in the retention of old customs and values. My great-grandparents would have assimilated more fully into the American way of life had they had the chance, as most of their children later had, to leave this Slavic-populated region.

Directly following their marriage, my grandparents had no choice but to remain in the coal mining community of Madera. During the next eight years, my grandmother bore three children; one in 1915, another in 1917, and a third in 1919. My grandfather continued his work in the coal mines. His job was to pick the coal loose by hand and load it into cars that were pulled out of the mines by mules. Besides the work being very laborious

Wedding portrait, Steven Kitko and Susanna Stroka, Madera, Pennsylvania, 1913.

and dangerous, there was little opportunity to move upward. My grandfather saved as much money as he could during his years as a coal miner in hope that one day he could get out of the mines and own a piece of land. In 1921, after thirteen years of mining coal, he had accumulated a savings of six to seven thousand dollars. It was an extraordinary accomplishment to have saved so much money in such difficult times. This accomplishment was made possible through his strong will and his determination to get out of the mines, own his own land, and give his children a better life. In 1921 his goal became a reality; he purchased a 125-acre farm in northeastern Ohio and also became a naturalized American citizen.

Owning their own farm was an opportunity neither of their parents had acquired and was atypical of Eastern European immigrant families of this period. My grandparents left behind their countrymen and old customs and settled in Greene, Ohio, a community populated by Protestants whose roots were in New England. It was at this point that the real Americanization process took place at a rapid pace. In order for my grandparents to utilize this opportunity to better their lives and the lives of their children, they attempted to become integrated into the local community. The first step was to learn to speak English. Evidence of the entire family's desire to integrate is that although the children were not restricted from speaking Slovak, none ever learned to speak it fluently. After a while, my grandparents earned the respect of people in the township and were described as honest, hard-working people. My grandparents had, in a sense, led the way for other Eastern European immigrants who later settled in this community.

During fifteen winters on the farm in Ohio, my grandmother, in the house and without a doctor, gave birth to seven more children. Because my grandparents placed such a high value on education, all nine of their children (one died shortly after birth of pneumonia) earned high school diplomas. Three of the children, including my father, were class valedictorian and one was class salutatorian. These achievements were high honors and proof of success on several levels: first, proof that the children were respected among their Protestant peers, teachers, and the rest of the community; second, that they assimilated well into the American way of life; finally, proof that they were in the process of making their parents' dream a reality—their educations marked the first step in advancing beyond the lives of their parents.

For the most part, the entire family assimilated well in America. Understandably, they held on to a few bonds with the Old World. As my great-grandparents were Catholic, so too were my grandparents, and they raised their children Catholic. When I asked my grandmother why she had so many children she replied, "Well, we were of the Catholic faith and we believed God wanted us to have children for they are the kingdom of heaven." My grandfather also held on to religious ties. He was frequently heard saying, "You do not have anything to lose if you believe in God." Their children also remained Catholic and raised their children in a Catholic environment. My grandparents' preservation of religious ties was not a barrier to the Americanization process but rather seemed to complement it.

America provided my grandparents with the opportunity to better their own lives and those of their children. In 1946 my grandfather sold his farm and purchased a larger 193-acre farm in the same community. In less than one generation he had worked his way out of poverty and left at his death a considerable estate. Unlike his father or uncles before him, he died not as a farm laborer, or a coal miner, but as a landowner—the very class of people who had exploited his family for generations in Austria-Hungary.

He insisted that his own children take advantage of the same opportunity that was afforded him in America. My grandparents sought to contribute to their children's success by conforming to American values and attitudes. Assimilation was the process by which they could give their children a better life than their own. As my father said, "They wanted to be Americans in every sense of the word." My grandparents became Americans and were respected by their fellow Americans. Their children were of the New World and there existed no Old World barriers that could serve to distinguish them from their peers. My grandparents had a dream identical to that of their parents—to provide a better life for their children. They were willing and did devote their lives to this end.

My grandparents' children made their dream a reality. All nine of the children graduated from high school. All four sons fought for America in World War II, the youngest dying on duty in 1944. The daughters kept the farm working while their brothers were away at war. The following is a brief description of their lives. It serves to illuminate the degree to which they advanced in the New World.

Ellen, the oldest daughter, married and spent her life as a mother of four and a school bus driver.

Joseph, my father, served twenty years in the Air Force and retired a lieutenant colonel. He received a bachelor's degree in economics. He then worked as a deputy probation officer for twelve years. I am one of his three children.

Frank retired from the Marines as a full Colonel. He received a Ph.D. in

Joseph Kitko, U.S. Air Force, 1953.

chemistry and is currently teaching at Kent State University in Ohio. He has four children.

David was a first lieutenant in the Air Force. He was killed at the age of twenty-three, flying a B-24 bomber during World War II. He never married.

Beatrice married and spent her life raising six children.

Matthew entered the service at seventeen, served in World War II, and later retired from the Navy. He is currently working for the federal government. He has five children.

Margaret received a bachelor's degree in education. She spent her life raising six children and teaching school.

Lucille received two years of college education, raised five children, and worked as a newspaper reporter.

Pamela received one year of college education. She was killed in an automobile accident at thirty-eight years of age. She never married.

Most of the children received some college education, which was not typical of children who grew up in their circumstances. Most of the daughters continued to work after marrying, again not usual for that time. Their lives testify to the value they placed on hard work and raising a family. Their values were thus similar to those of their parents, but because of their parents' efforts, they were able to excel beyond their parents' social and economic position.

In my father I cannot see any trace of the Old World. He seems to represent every value upon which this country was founded. He is hard-working, conservative, and a "rugged individualist." My father has, however, retained one value that can be traced back to his forebears. It is the same value that prompted my great-grandfather to leave Austria-Hungary and make America his family's home. My great-grandfather had a dream—to provide a better life for his children. My father, two generations later, held on to this dream. He spent his life devoted to giving his children a better life. As he and his brothers and sisters made his parents' dream a reality, my brothers and I have made his dream a reality.

By devoting his life to furthering mine, my father has inspired me to do the same for my children. Although I cannot provide a significantly better economic life for my children, I will devote my life to them. I would never relinquish a value meaningful enough to have survived so many generations. I will attempt to make sure that this value—the only one I feel to be connected to my roots—survives many more generations. As significant as it was to my forebears, so it shall be to me.

Rachel Koch (SUNY Binghamton 1990)

The Loss of My Family's Ethnic Ties and the Strengthening of Their American Identities

Reflecting on her childhood, my grandmother Julia Koch remembers fondly the time she spent in the Old Country and most of her experiences once she moved to the United States. Born on April 25, 1906, on the small island of Rhodes, my grandmother was the youngest of seven children in the Capuya family of Spanish Jews. Leaving her beautiful tourist island was sad for my grandmother, but she also looked forward to the opportunities and freedoms the United States had to offer. Her immigration experience followed the pattern of many other Jewish immigrants of that period. My grandmother, however, was more fortunate than most in that, comparatively speaking, her journey to America was very smooth because of her ability to adjust to American life.

Rhodes is a beautiful island located between Greece and Turkey, with a temperate climate and a tourist season in the summer months. Many of the Spanish Jews fled from Spain to Rhodes, Italy, Turkey, Holland, and Denmark at the time of the Spanish Inquisition. That is how my grandmother's family found themselves residing in Rhodes. At this time Rhodes was under control of the Turkish government. The Spanish Jews led a comfortable life in Rhodes mixed among the Turks and the Greeks. My grandmother's family did, however, resent the fact that the Turks never elected any of the Jews to political office. My grandmother felt they had a right to representation. Then, in 1912, the Italian government gained control of Rhodes and treated its people with more respect than the Turks had done.

The economy of Rhodes was good for most of the people living there.

My grandmother's family led a middle-class life and enjoyed a good position in society. Her father owned a small shoe business and had a few employees. Rhodes at this time had many small family businesses. There were many small shops that carried dry goods, leather, and basic necessities. The economic opportunities, however, dwindled as the number of families grew.

My great-grandfather's shoe business did well, but there were not many business options for his sons. My grandmother had three brothers, Joe, Albert, and Victor, and three sisters, Selma, Rachel, and Laura. They all attended French schools because my great-grandparents believed strongly in educating their children, especially the boys. Joe, Albert, and Victor also went to Paris to study so they could advance themselves in business. The sisters found some lower-skilled jobs after they completed their schooling, but it was more difficult for the brothers to start businesses because there was no need for any new ones. At this time the Jewish people believed strongly in the importance of males in the family and their ability to earn a living to support the family. That is why my great-grandparents became concerned about their sons' future job prospects if they were to remain in Rhodes. At this time the family started to reevaluate their position and the opportunities left for them on Rhodes.

Commonly in the early 1900s and 1910s people from Rhodes began to immigrate to Africa or the United States in search of economic opportunity. My great-grandfather thought a lot about these options while thinking of his sons' futures. They ruled out going to Africa because of the hot weather and the problems with tsetse flies and malaria. They did, however, hear many good things about the United States. It was a big country and they heard it was quite liberal and independent. They believed it would be a change for the better, living in a democratic society where Jews could run for political office if they wanted. Many people left Rhodes for America and wrote back about the unlimited economic opportunities it had to offer. They also wrote that although one had to work hard, one could earn a decent living. Others went as far as to say that people in America were so rich that one could find money on the streets.

Running out of options in Rhodes, my great-grandfather and two of his sons, Joe and Albert, left in 1910 to take up residence in the United States. They hoped to send for the rest of the family once they established themselves. They settled in Seattle, Washington, where Albert and Joe went to school and my great-grandfather opened a postcard store. Unfortunately, being a new immigrant and not speaking English, my great-grandfather misunderstood the American legalities of running a business. The man that sold the store to him did not explain that he had to have a lease to run the store. My great-grandfather had invested a lot of his savings into the store and it was taken away from him because he did not have a lease. Broken-hearted, my great-grandfather packed his bags and returned home to Rhodes after only nine months in the United States and reopened his shoe business. My grandmother's brothers, Joe and Albert, remained in the United States to finish their education. They were able to attend school and work on the side to support themselves. Eventually they settled in New York. It was pointless for the brothers to return to Rhodes because there were no job opportunities there for them. Then, in 1916 my grandmother's other brother Victor joined Joe and Albert in the United States.

After World War I, the rest of the Capuya family decided it was time to reunite the family and joined Joe, Albert, and Victor in the United States. They were luckier than most because they had the money to travel comfortably. Their journey over was much easier and more pleasant than that for many immigrant families. They boarded a ship, the *Patrea,* where they traveled in second class for ten days, not including stopovers, before they reached the United States. Their first stop was in Naples for one week to pick up passengers. My grandmother was in her early teens so she remained on board ship with her parents while her sisters took this opportunity to sightsee. They made a couple of other stops, and overall it was a nice trip. They had their own cabin, unlike many others cramped into steerage quarters, and they were fed well. Even with ship regulations, many immigrants were stuffed into crowded quarters and given stale, unappetizing food. Fortunately, my grandmother's family had no such problems.

My grandmother's brothers were settled in the United States and had jobs, making it much easier for my grandmother's family to enter. My grandmother's brother Joe had met and married a woman named Rose and was living in the Bronx. Albert and Victor were also living in the Bronx, boarding with people. Joe and Albert had papers prepared for the rest of the family and met them as they docked at Ellis Island. The government allowed them to enter without much hassle because they had working relatives in the United States and would not become a burden on society. They did, however, have to submit to the doctor's physical at Ellis Island to make sure they were not bringing over any contagious diseases.

The Capuya family eventually settled in a Spanish Jewish enclave in Brooklyn, New York. They found a beautiful nine-room house to live in. Albert and Victor still boarded with people separately, but Joe and his wife, Rose, and daughter, Claire, came to live with my grandmother's family. Living among their own people really helped them adjust to life in the United States because they did not yet know the English language. However, my grandmother's family was well educated. They knew French, Spanish, and Italian, which helped make up for their inability to speak English.

My grandmother's brother Joe previously had written his family wonderful letters about life in America, but when they got there it was a big disappointment. My grandmother thought that when they arrived they were going to find successful brothers and a wonderful life. It would have been this way, but my grandmother's family hated Joe's wife, Rose, and Rose made them miserable. In following with Jewish customs and the belief in family, they had to be nice to Rose even when she did horrible things. My grandmother's family was very insulted when they first arrived in America and Rose greeted them in a bathrobe in a dirty house, with no supper prepared for them after a long journey. After what they were accustomed to in Rhodes, this was a big disappointment. My great-grandfather came to the United States with savings, and Rose took a lot of it and spent it foolishly, and there was nothing that could be done about it. Other than Rose's relationship with the family, my grandmother said they liked living in the United States.

The family then moved to Harlem in a six-room apartment and really found their niche in American society. Again my grandmother's family was surrounded by Spanish Jews, which made them very comfortable. Rachel and Laura found jobs, and together with my great-grandfather's savings and the money of my grandmother's brothers, Albert and Victor, the family was able to do well. My grandmother was then able to attend high school. My grandmother was fortunate because not many women at this time were able to attend school past the lower elementary grades. Her education was interrupted for one year, though, when she came down with tuberculosis and had to spend a year in the country mountains to recuperate. Then she went back to school and eventually graduated from high school.

Again the family moved, this time to the Bronx among more people of their ethnic background. Then the depression hit. Luckily they were able to find jobs. Victor found work with a shipping company, while Albert was employed by the Metropolitan Life Insurance Company. My grandmother's family was fortunate; they were not rich, but always made enough money for a decent living. They also felt very little oppression living among other Spanish Jews. My grandmother claims it was very safe when she was younger. There were no thefts or killings. She always felt safe using the subway, and streets where she lived were kept quite clean. She was always proud to call herself an American citizen.

In the 1930s my grandmother met and married the American-born son of Russian immigrants, Louis Koch. My grandparents established their

Julia Capuya, grandmother of Rachel Koch (left), and Mildred Birnbaum, New York City, 1935.

Julia Koch, with her brother Victor Capuya and her granddaughter Rachel Koch, 1991.

own home and were able to live a decent life. They still valued the importance of family, and really felt at home in American society. Things were looking up for my grandmother, and in 1941 my father, Robert Koch, was born. He was raised in the Jewish tradition, but living in the United States he was not as close to his mixed Russian and Spanish heritage as his parents were. Like so many second-generation Americans, my father became fully a part of American culture. In actuality, his parents no longer regarded themselves as Spanish or Russian; they thought of themselves as Americans, and they transmitted this belief to my father. Not that my grandparents did not remember or value their heritages, but their sense of being U.S. citizens far outweighed their loyalty to their old countries.

Then my father met and married my mother, Joyce Silka, and it seemed as if there was no longer anything holding together our ethnic identity. My mother was Irish, German, Scottish, and English. Combined with my father's Spanish and Russian heritage, I really do not feel a part of a distinct culture other than American. We also faced a new problem; my mother was Protestant, while my father was Jewish. Living among the many different ethnic groups and religions in the United States for many years, my parents and their families felt no need for their differences to deter their marriage. As we were growing up, my sister and I were mildly exposed to (but not really educated in) both Protestantism and Judaism. Thus we never felt strongly about either one. As a result, we felt left out of a part of our heritage. Because of this sense of loss, I have decided to raise my own children when I get married under the religion of my husband. In American society today, since many of us have no ethnic identity other than American, I feel it is important to have a religion with which to identify.

In tracing my roots, I have discovered a lot about my family's beliefs and how important it is to keep in touch with our past. As the generations succeed each other, we need to remind our children about their roots so they too can feel a distinct part of society. My grandmother's story is not typical. She did not suffer much and had an easy time traveling to America and adapting to American society. My grandmother's family was typical, however, in that family members came to America separately, helping each other settle and adjust to American life. They also lived near people of their ethnic descent, valued the closeness of family, and considered it an honor and a privilege to call themselves Americans. I have learned a great deal from my grandmother and really regret not making an effort sooner to learn more about my family's past. From my parents' generation onward, though, I believe most of us will truly regard ourselves as Americans, an evolving ethnic group, something we can be proud of.

Karen A. Gryga (SUNY Binghamton 1992)

What's a Tyrolean? The Immigration of Mario Leonardi to America

Well, Solvay was known as Little Tyrol. We had most of the streets. Caroline. Freeman. Lamont. Williams Street. They were all Tyroleans living there—and they all worked down at Solvay Process. . . . If you're a Tyrolean, you are a Tyrolean. You know it and you let people know it.

Rita Cominolli, Smokestacks Allegro

Solvay is a small village approximately one mile west of Syracuse, New York, located in central New York State. Begun as an small industrial town and populated largely by immigrants working at Solvay Process and by the engineers and corporate executives of Solvay Process, Solvay still survives as a little village, although the plant was shut down in 1986. Solvay Process, later incorporated into the Allied Chemical Corporation, was the first soda ash plant in the United States. Built by Rowland Hazard, Solvay Process took its name from the process in which sodium carbonate, a widely used alkali in industry, was produced, a method profitably developed by the Solvay brothers of Belgium.[1] At first a largely Irish settlement, Solvay began to draw Tyrolean immigrants in the late 1880s, and through the processes of chain migration created a strong Tyrolean and Italian community that still exists today. When anyone asks me what my ethnic background is, I always respond, "Polish and . . . well, Tyrolean. Do you know what that is?" and I am always asked to explain what "Tyrolean" means. It is because my mother's father, Mario Leonardi, chose to settle in Solvay that I have a sense of what Tyrolean is, and how it is different from either an Italian or an Austrian background.

The Tyrol at one time was considered to be the land on either side of the pass now connecting Austria and Italy, the Brenner Pass. The Tyrol family held this land as an independent domain within Austria until the French took it over in 1802. Austria regained it only to have the French retake the land and cede it to Bavaria. Through this back and forth battle,

Solvay Process Company, viewed from across the Erie Canal, 1913. (Courtesy Solvay Public Library)

the "Tyroleans" began to develop a fierce sense of nationality and began referring to themselves as Tyroleans or Trentini, the latter in reference to one of the provinces (Trentino) in the Tyrol (the other being Alto Adige). When Austria again regained control of the Tyrol, some Tyroleans considered themselves Austrian, but those living in the southernmost portion of the Tyrol often felt a closer connection with northern Italy. In 1919 Italy took over Trentino, and in 1923 Trentino formally became an Italian province. The self-proclaimed differences between Northern Italians and Southern Italians were given yet another dimension with these people from the North. Whether calling themselves Austrian, Italian, Tyrolean, Trentini, or later, American, these people of the Tyrol immigrated mainly to a few specific areas in the United States, and in the example of Solvay, created a Tyrolean-centered town.[2]

My grandfather Mario Leonardi, born on March 6, 1889 in the town of Preore in the province of Trentino, was one of three children of Maria Ballardini and Giuseppe Leonardi. (The other two children were Sebastino and Leone, about whom my mother knew very little other than their existence.) My grandfather used to tell my mother how he went into the woods of the Tyrol to chop wood, sometimes crossing the Austrian border, and in the process managed to pick up a few German phrases. (Including, of course, *Sprechen Sie Deutsch?* which would make my mom laugh every time he said it.) In looking through Mario's belongings, I found a small ceramic pipe with a battlefield scene painted on it with the words *Ricordo de mio servissio Mario Leonardi, 1910* ["Remember my service," signifying his period of military service.] Although he never spoke of it with my mother, it is possible that my grandfather, at that time twenty-one years old, had been involved in the service in the Tyrol where German-speaking and Italian-speaking Tyroleans were often fighting to determine which nation would have control over them, Austria or Italy. A few years later, during World War I, my grandfather decided to travel to America for the first time.

In either 1913 or 1914 my grandfather traveled with other Tyrolean countrymen (and they were exclusively men) from the Tyrol to America to work in a Pennsylvania coal mine. After the coal mine closed he and his *paesano,* Giulio Leonardi, probably a distant relation if any, traveled to Solvay. Both Giulio and Mario obtained jobs at Solvay Process (found for them by the son of the president of Solvay Process when Giulio played the harmonica and my grandfather played the guitar at a dance), and much to Giulio's glee, pushed two Southern Italians out of jobs in the process.[3] Tyroleans in Solvay were seen as good workers not only because they were

Karen Gryga's maternal grandfather, Mario Leonardo, ca. 1913.

Mario Leonardo (left), ca. 1913.

reliable, but also because they tended to be somewhat passive in that they did not make any trouble.[4] Giulio and Mario worked until 1919–20 when they both returned to the Tyrol. However, Mario seemed to be going back to arrange for marriage, because he returned to Solvay in 1921 and was married to Elodia Leonardi (no relation) in 1923.

From my grandfather's passport, I determined that he sailed on the SS *Corsican* from Le Havre on January 13, 1921, reaching Le Havre by way of Venice, which he left five weeks earlier. Because I could not find my grandmother Elodia's passport, I am unsure as to whether she traveled with him or with other *paesani*. Most Tyrolean women came to America between 1920 and 1935, and it is likely that if Elodia and Mario did not come together, she would have had no problem finding others with whom to travel.[5] Elodia, the daughter of Modesta Scalfi and Domenico Leonardi, was born on May 25, 1895, one of eight children, and would have known or would have been related to a number of people who were emigrating to America, and possibly Solvay at the same time.

Scratched in my grandfather's passport are the names of people he had been referred to in Solvay as *paesani*, which literally meant people from the same village. However, as one Tyrolean explained, "the further [*sic*] away you are from your village, the wider the area you consider to encompass a *paesano*."[6] These people were the Furlettis who lived on Williams Street in Solvay, a central part of the Tyrolese settlement. Many of these people, including my grandfather, came from villages in the Val Giudicarie in Trentino.[7] People would congregate in these areas to socialize, and typically the men would spend a good part of the time in the saloons. Although my mother said my grandfather had never been a heavy drinker, not one to take the traditional glass of wine with dinner or return home after work tipsy, I did find a handwritten recipe for *16 galoni grappi*, or homemade whiskey, that Tyroleans as well as Italians were known to make. My grandfather had also told my mother of a time when he had been in a speakeasy during Prohibition and was given whiskey that literally made all the hair on his head stand straight up. This experience may have put a permanent damper on his desire for homemade whiskey.

Elodia and Mario Leonardi were married on July 19, 1923, when Mario was thirty-four and Elodia twenty-eight, in St. Cecilia's Church, formerly an Irish parish that was now becoming more Tyrolean and Italian. My grandfather was not an overly religious man; in fact, my mother rarely remembers him attending mass, as most Tyrolean men did not, although he did reminisce about his altar boy days "ringing the bells" in Preore. She remembers him instead working around the house on Freeman Avenue that he and Elodia had purchased in 1925, fixing something, tending to his beautiful garden, and even pouring the concrete for the sidewalks around the house. My mother does remember celebrating the *sagra,* the annual feast day for the saint of the village from which the celebrating group had emigrated. On one Sunday in the summer months their friends would gather to celebrate and eat *polenta* (a dish made of cornmeal, served with chicken and gravy by Tyroleans), *torte* (a hard almond cake), and *capon* (a mixture of Swiss chard, garlic, dry bread, and cheese wrapped in grape leaves). Even if one did not attend mass frequently, the *sagra* was not something to miss. The Southern Italians began the tradition of celebrating the Feast of the Assumption on 15 August annually, but the Tyroleans retained their celebrations nonetheless.

Ethnic rivalries in the town were not limited to Tyrolean-Italian rivalries. The house I live in now on Freeman Avenue is the same house that my grandfather bought for $5,500 from one Joseph O'Brien. Freeman was one of the streets at that time where more and more Tyroleans were coming to live. The Irish tended to move out of areas in Solvay once Tyroleans or Italians moved in. This is partially the reason why the large Irish group that had been in Solvay gradually moved to the west side of Syracuse, now called the Tipperary Hill area.[8] My grandfather once told stories of working for the Department of Public Works before he was hired at Solvay Process. He was incredibly proud of this work because he was building roads that became part of the country and were used by many people. It seems that he worked on one road crew where there were not enough shovels to go around and men were expected to share. My grandfather claimed that he was hard at work even when the supervisor was not around, but the other men were content to stand idle. However, as soon as the foreman returned, one of the workers, specifically identified as an Irishman, grabbed my grandfather's shovel and proceeded to pretend he had been working all along. My grandfather seemed to think this was typical of Irish workers.

Although he did take pride in being Tyrolean, my grandfather also Americanized to some extent. He learned to speak and to read English, and read the Syracuse newspapers at home daily while speaking to my mother and uncle in English. He received his certificate of literacy in 1931, one year after my mother was born. He worked with other Tyroleans and was a member of the Societa Tiolese Dimuto Soccorro Franz Joseph, which had an emblem with both the American and Austrian flags on it, and which took its name from Franz Joseph, the Austrian emperor from 1848 to 1916.[9] Limited to residents of Onondaga county, the society was a mutual benefit society of Tyroleans only. With one-dollar quarterly dues, this society helped when members were unable to work due to sickness and allowed them to survive in these times. My grandfather did not, however, join the Tyrol Club, which was geared more toward socializing. My mother said Mario was more apt to keep to himself, again working in the garden or on the house. He also enjoyed going to the movies, both for the news shown before the main feature and the movie itself, and enjoyed going alone. Not a heavy drinker, he tended to stay away from the traditional socializing in the saloon.

I have not written extensively about my grandmother Elodia because she died at the early age of forty-eight and my mother does not remember a great deal about her. One fond memory she does recall clearly is that of my grandmother singing along with the opera every Saturday. She had not been a chronically ill woman, but giving birth to Bruno in 1925, and my mother in 1932, between which time she gave birth to a boy, Lino, and a girl, Nita Margaret (in 1928 and then in 1929) who both died, took its toll. Elodia's death created a void in the family that my mother, twelve years old at the time, was expected to fill. Relegated to doing the cooking and cleaning around the house for her father (her brother Bruno had joined the service), she was given support by a neighborhood family friend, Rosa Bella. Rosa was my grandmother's age and also from the Old World, and so she tended to espouse the idea of my mother as housekeeper rather than anything else. My mother in reminiscing told me how Rosa herself used to cook dinner for the Bella family and perhaps a few guests and then sit in the corner by herself while everyone else ate, because that was what women were supposed to do.

My grandfather worked at Solvay Process for thirty-six years as a laborer, then retired and began collecting his pension. My mother said that while she was growing up, her father continually worried about his health and was often going to doctors, possibly as a result of continually dealing with soda ash at the factory. After his retirement, he continued to do his usual work around the house. When my mother married in 1955 and was working at the telephone company as a service representative, she and my father, Joseph Gryga, moved to the north side of Syracuse, and my uncle and his wife moved in with my grandfather. When my uncle moved out of the house, and my grandfather seemed to be in waning health, my parents moved back into the house to live with my grandfather. After my mother gave birth to my brother and sister, Paul and Jeanette, in 1957 and 1959, respectively, my grandfather became increasingly ill, creating another responsibility for my mother. My grandfather was able to enjoy some time with his grandchildren, and was able to take my brother mushroom picking in areas that are now completely settled around my home, but my brother and sister have few memories of him because he died when they were young.

My grandfather died in 1963, but the Tyrolean traditions for my family did not all die with him. We continue to eat *polenta,* Tyrolean, not Italian style, and my mother is teaching me to make it for myself. Although we celebrate Polish Christmas vigilia and Polish Easter, my mother continually reminds us of the Tyrolean traditions, and we tend to eat more Tyrolean than Polish foods throughout the year. Because I grew up in a town where there were an abundance of people who became livid if you called them Italian rather than Tyrolean, I learned to be proud of my different heritage and even came to enjoy having to explain what exactly it was to people who did not understand or who were quick to label those of us from Solvay "cat-eaters." (This moniker developed when it was rumored that Tyroleans ate cats during the depression when they were desperate for food. Personally, I have never eaten a cat nor have I known anyone who ate a cat, although I am sure in desperation people may eat anything. At least they did not resort to eating each other.)

Although I do not profess to know everything about my ancestors, and I am sure there are things the Tyroleans may have done that I would not agree with, I am proud to acknowledge my Tyrolean ancestry, and I am proud to be associated with someone of my grandfather's character. I choose to see myself as an American of Polish descent because I enjoy the customs and learning the history of my ancestors. I also think it is important, especially in the face of continuing immigration, that I acknowledge the fact that although I am "American" my ancestors were once foreigners here, and were treated like outsiders themselves. In the words of Tyrolean immigrant Oreste Chemotti, "only the Indian is American citizen, that isn't a foreigner. Otherwise I don't care what nationality you are, you[r] father, or your grandfather, I don't care who it was, they all come from over across."[10]

Notes

1. Rita Cominolli, *Smokestacks Allegro: The Story of Solvay, a Remarkable Industrial/Immigrant Village (1880–1920)* (New York: Center for Migration Studies, 1990), 3.
2. Ibid., chap. 2, especially 22–24.

3. For parallel evidence of ethnic rivalries in Solvay, see Cominolli, *Smokestacks Allegro,* 79.

4. Ibid., 100.

5. Ibid., 61.

6. Ibid., 57.

7. Ibid., 56.

8. Ibid., 83.

9. Ibid., 128.

10. Ibid., 77.

Marc Turetzky (UC San Diego 1984)

Turetzky Family Assimilation: From Grandparents to Father to Me

Assimilation is defined as a process by which people take up and are absorbed into a culture. This essay discusses the migration of my paternal grandparents from Russia to the United States and their rejection of assimilation. It tells how they managed to cling steadfastly to their old-world ideals of religion and family, and how their son (my father) and our family have assimilated in this country.

I know little about the experience of my Grandfather Turetzky in traveling to this country; I focus instead on my Grandmother Tillie and her family's struggle. Grandmother Tillie lived in a Russian shtetl called Brodi with her mother, a brother and a sister, and her father. Tillie's family was forced to leave Brodi in 1918 because of religious persecution and the violent assaults on their town by Russian Cossacks. She recalls hiding in an oven built into the wall and seeing the Russian cavalry (Cossacks) ride into the shtetl and kill babies by throwing them in the air and catching them on their swords like a shish kebab.

In 1918 Tillie and her family walked from Brodi to Warsaw, starting a journey that would take them to the United States by 1921. On their way, though, they stopped at a shtetl of a relative in order for Tillie's mother to give birth to a child. The poverty was so great that the shtetl had no doctor, and my great-grandmother's baby was born under the kitchen table. This scene is reminiscent of what happened in Marie Hall Ets's book to the immigrant Rosa when she gave birth to her child.[1] After a month-long stay at the shtetl in Warsaw, the family pressed on to their destination,

Brussels, in Belgium. In all, Tillie's family had walked hundreds of miles to finally reach Brussels. Great-grandmother Goldie's feet were never the same after the walk, but her strength, courage, and religious faith helped her family on the journey.

Brussels proved to be a temporary residence, and in 1921 they took a boat to the United States. Not one person in the family spoke a word of English, but the oldest daughter was already living in New York and was ready to help. On the boat, the family was booked into steerage, which was below the deck, crowded and unsanitary. In order to eat, Tillie would catch fish off the boat and trade them for eggs with the richer passengers to achieve more of a balanced diet.

Finally, they docked in America, at Ellis Island. Immediately, they moved to the Lower East Side on Hester Street. Great-grandmother, Grandmother Tillie, the two sisters, and the brother went to work in the garment district in sweatshops. Tillie sewed dresses by machine, working twelve to fourteen hours per day, six days a week. After three and a half years of hard labor and living in tenement apartments, the family spent a summer on a farm in Preston, a town near Norwich, Connecticut.

Preston was the town in which Tillie met Isador Turetzky, my grandfather. Isador was the oldest son of a father who had taken his family to America about the same time as Grandmother Tillie.

His father was very religious and was the equivalent of a deacon in the Norwich synagogue. He owned and operated a general store in which Isador worked. Isador was brought up by his father in a very orthodox, religious way, studying the Torah extensively. Isador also had enough time to master six languages and was influenced greatly by his uncle, Abraham Negevitsky, an old rabbi who used to visit his home. Isador studied Hebrew with this great rabbi and was inspired at a young age to study the Torah for life. In 1926 Isador Turetzky was married to Tillie, and in 1932 my father, Bertram Jay Turetzky, was born. There was another boy, Seymor Benjamin Turetzky, and thus the Turetzky family became complete. The household was the typical old-world, orthodox Jewish household, following all dietary laws to the letter, meaning that family members ate only kosher foods.

The Turetzkys celebrated all Jewish holidays and lived in a very patriarchal setting. Consequently, the family was built around the father, Isador. The setting was Old World, in that even the great-grandmother lived with the family. Although Isador was very religious and studied the Torah every chance he had, he did assimilate slightly in that he owned and operated his own gasoline station for thirty-five years. He was thus considered a busi-

Wedding portrait, Isador and Tillie Turetzky, Norwich, Connecticut, 1926.

nessman in America. An important point to make, though, was that Isador did not consider himself an American businessman because his heart was never truly in that work. His heart lay with the Torah and with his family. He was much like the old-world father in Yezierska's *Bread Givers,* but Isador was never such a tyrant.[2] He clung steadfastly to his roots in the Old World and was a disciplinarian, but in a kind and understanding way, my dad has always told me.

Some of Isador's happier moments in life were spent discussing the Torah and the Bible with Father Francis Baldwin, a Catholic priest, who would consult and discuss translations of the Old Testament with Grandfather. He also loved to discuss the Torah with his two sons, Bert and Seymor.

Another important point about the worldview of Isador Turetzky was his great respect for higher education. He always told his two sons that they had to get their education and that this was not negotiable. A college education was thus the destiny for Seymor Benjamin and Bertram Turetzky. They were both helped through college as much as Isador could contribute—my father at Hartt College and Benjamin at M.I.T. He helped my father tremendously to fight his way through school and finally earn his degree in music, because there was a time when my Dad needed the help (a kick in the a—!). He always told Bertram, "You can be anything you want to be if you work hard enough and you can reach heaven through being a good person and having faith in G-d."

My father believes in God, but is not a conventionally religious person. He went to Hebrew School and studied the Torah, and eventually was Bar Mitzvahed. But by the age of sixteen, he knew in his heart that he was simply not devoted to religion because he loved music and wanted eventually to become a musician. Coming from a very strict and orthodox family, this was something of a problem. Neither his father nor his mother was particularly assimilated into the American way of life. They were still Old World. With my father, though, the process of assimilation was slowly beginning.

His first act of assimilating occurred when he was thirteen. Isador and Tillie wanted their son to take up either the violin or the piano. Instead, Bertram chose to play the banjo. This was a shock to his parents. They saw it as a move toward assimilation, in that the banjo was an "American" instrument. Thomas Jefferson had even named it the banjo, so it had to be an American instrument, thought Isador. Dad had even unconsciously thought that he could become more American by playing the banjo, having read that Mark Twain considered the banjo a quintessentially American instrument.

Another huge disappointment to his parents was the decision Bertram made to become a musician. This caused a rift between Tillie and her son that only healed when he became a professor in 1958, at the University of Hartford.

The final, and probably most important, incident for my father was marrying my mother, a non-Jew, and moving away from his parents. The marriage to a non-Jew was a jolt to the family and Grandmother was very sick for two weeks after the trauma of the marriage. These developments were critical parts of my father's assimilation; he did not become what his parents had expected (a lawyer or a doctor) and he had married a person not of the same faith. He had become, in their minds, American.

My mother, Nancy Turetzky, converted to Judaism after thirteen years of marriage. That event, coupled with my brother Gerry's Bar Mitzvah, made Grandmother Tillie happy at last with that aspect of her son's life. Bertram had kept the old traditions intact and thus, in Tillie's eyes, her son hadn't completely assimilated the new ways.

When he moved away from his parents and the Jewish ghettos of the East Coast to the non-Jewish neighborhood of Del Mar, California, this could be seen as his final move toward assimilation. But as he gets older, Dad feels the need to read and learn more about Jewish culture, poets, their music, and so on. He seems to have a longing to reach back to his roots, as if he, like the author Anzia Yezierska, had somehow gotten caught between two worlds, the old days in the Jewish ghettos and his present days in Del Mar. I wonder if he has not gone full circle, from the ghetto and out, and now, maybe, back to his roots again.

Finally, this story of assimilation leads to me—a third-generation student attending UCSD and striving for rewards in the field of business. How have I been affected by the plight of my grandparents in their journey to America? Their struggle in sweatshops and living on the Lower East Side and hoping for something better for their lives and future Turetzkys' lives makes me think hard about where I am today and where I might have ended up. I would rather not think of an alternative life because I simply appreciate the life I have been given by my parents and grandparents. The fact that I am Jewish makes me all the more proud. A few years back, though, I never would have said I was proud of my Jewish heritage. I was embarrassed to tell anyone I attended Hebrew school or the synagogue because I did not want to be laughed at. I thought that to deny the fact that I was Jewish would make me normal, like everyone else. As I grew up, though, I found that being like everyone else was not necessarily what I wanted. Being Jewish was something that made me different from most of the people I have been associated with. I came to understand and appreciate our very rich family heritage and, through the help of Third World Studies 7B, I believe that my understanding of what my grandparents went through to reach this country has been enhanced. It was extraordinary what my grandparents fought—poverty, hunger, possible death—while holding onto their faith and religion, and finally reaching the American shores to start a new life.

My life has been affected by my grandparents and, obviously, my parents. I was brought to Del Mar, California, by them, in order for us (my older brother, younger sister, and me) to have a chance at a better life than they had. I consider myself to be an American Jew assimilated completely into this country. I grasp, work, and dream for a successful future, but I can now look to the past and appreciate what it means to be a stranger in a new country and hold steadfast to one's old-world religion and beliefs like Isador and Tillie did. I can also understand better the fact that my father feels that he must continue to keep at least some of the old-world traditions alive. I respect and understand this and accept that I, too, am Jewish and that I will keep the Jewish faith alive within my future family. It is something that I simply feel I owe to my heritage.

Notes

1. Marie Hall Ets, *Rosa: The Life of an Italian Immigrant* (Minneapolis: University of Minnesota Press, 1970), chap. 20.
2. Anzia Yezierska, *Bread Givers* (1925; reprint, New York: Persea Books, 1975).

Stephanie A. Courtney (SUNY Binghamton 1989)

Changing Worlds: The Immigration Experiences of My Paternal Grandparents

I consider myself fortunate when researching the lives of my relatives who immigrated to this country because of the excellent oral testimony of my paternal grandmother, MaryKate Courtney. She immigrated to America in 1920, a prosperous time directly after World War I, and is, I think, a shining example of the "immigrant success story." This essay discusses the immigration experiences of MaryKate and her late husband, PJ Courtney, as well as their lives in America.

MaryKate lived with her large family in a peaceful section of southwestern Ireland on the farmlands around the village of Drumshambo in Leetram County. The farmlands that surrounded the central villages were called townlands, and MaryKate lived on a small farm on the townland of Curaghy. She was the oldest girl in a family of four boys and five girls, in which two of the children died very young. Being the eldest female in a poor family of that size required a lot of responsibility from her. At the age of eight, MaryKate was cooking, sewing, watching the children, and doing demanding household chores as well. Her mother worked around the house, tended a small vegetable garden, and raised chickens and geese. Her father was a farmer as well as a shoemaker so that even in the hardest times, MaryKate remembers, everyone in her family always had a pair of shoes. MaryKate has fond memories of both of her parents, but remembers them, especially her father, as strict Catholics who would keep a very close eye on the social lives of their children.

She recalls a time when she and her two sisters, Margaret and Suzy, attended a dance at a neighbor's house. Because the girls were having so much fun, they lost track of time and stayed out too late the night before an early morning mass. Their father walked across farm fields to the dance in the dead of night with his belt in his hand and quietly but sternly announced that it was time to go home. Suzy, humiliated, was muttering the whole way home, and even picked up a rock to throw at him, but was restrained by her other two sisters. In any event, the combination of the hardship of farm life along with the stifling strictures of religion were major influences that prompted MaryKate and her brothers and sisters to emigrate.

It was pretty much MaryKate's decision to immigrate to America in 1920 at the age of twenty. When her mother was about MaryKate's age, she had gone to America to work as a live-in servant in Connecticut for several years, but then returned to Ireland to marry after making some money. MaryKate had wanted to be rid of the farming life for a long time, and she was anxious to have an opportunity to make her own fortune and to send her family anything she could spare from her wages. She saved up enough to pay for her own ticket, and with a cousin and a group of friends from Drumshambo, she left from Dublin on a White Star Line ship called the *Camernia* headed for Ellis Island. The ocean voyage she describes as "wonderful," with all of them full of the optimism of youth. She also remembers the thrill she felt when she first saw the Statue of Liberty.

She describes the actual inspection process at Ellis Island as "not bad," because the group she traveled with had the bulk of their paperwork done in Dublin. They were also examined by an Irish doctor in Dublin who had given them all a clean bill of health so they did not have to be examined by a doctor at Ellis Island. MaryKate's cousin met her directly at the dock to take her to her house in Queens. She stayed with her cousin for two weeks before taking a job as a domestic servant for a wealthy American family. For the first few years of her life in America, she worked as a domestic servant for wealthy families of English American descent. The families were always happy with her work and gave excellent references whenever she needed them. She continued working as a domestic servant for most of the 1920s until she got married. She considers herself very lucky that she immigrated when she did. The years following World War I were prosperous up until the depression. Jobs were plentiful and wages were high. She made enough money to pay for the transportation of two of her sisters, Margaret and Elizabeth, and even had enough to send home to help out there.

Oftentimes people who came from the same areas in Ireland would host dances or other social events for fellow Irishmen and women. People from

MaryKate Courtney's passport picture, 1920.

Leitram County, MaryKate's home, hosted one of these dances, which is where MaryKate met her future husband, PJ Courtney.

Although no one is really sure when PJ was born, most agree that it was probably 1886. The Courtney family owned a rather successful farm in Ulster, now located in Northern Ireland. To make money during World War I, they also raised and sold horses to English soldiers. However, when Ireland split in 1922, Ulster ended up three miles north of the border. Since the majority of the Northern counties in Ireland, including Ulster, were Protestant, an agreement was made in which the British continued their economic control over Northern Ireland, thus ensuring the British total control over the Irish. This agreement disgusted PJ. He felt that the Irish sold out to the British. The fact that Ulster was only three miles from the border that separated the North from the South only made him feel more bitter. These factors were the influences that pushed PJ to join the underground resistance against the British, which was in no way affiliated with the IRA.

There is one story about PJ that I love to hear. One day when PJ was carrying supplies to some of the rebels, he spotted several English soldiers heading toward him a little way down the road. Quickly, he put the supplies on a bank of a nearby stream and walked on. The soldiers searched and questioned him, but finding nothing out of the ordinary, they continued on their way. However, while PJ was being interrogated, he saw out of the corner of his eye the bandages floating down stream. Fortunately, the soldiers did not notice, for if they had, PJ surely would have been put in jail. When he left Ireland it was not under the same conditions as MaryKate. The British were searching for him.

After getting married in 1927, PJ and MaryKate moved into a relatively modern apartment in the then nice South Bronx in a mostly Irish and Italian neighborhood. MaryKate remembers how impressed she was when she found out that their new apartment had elevators. PJ made good money as a stonecutter for building construction during the predepression years. They also had four children: Jimmy and Peggy in the late twenties, and Theresa and William, my father, in the early thirties.

During the depression PJ still supported a family of six as a stonecutter for street building through the PWA, a program designed by Roosevelt's New Deal Administration. For a long time after the depression, MaryKate worked as a waitress at a restaurant for employees of a large corporate bank.

My father says that there were some Irish traditions that were evident in their household. Their religion was strictly observed, and going to mass was a top priority. Also, every Sunday afternoon they would have a large supper, as was the custom back in Ireland and still is today. All four of their children went to parochial school as well. My father also tells me that his family did not encounter many outward forms of racism because of the heavily Irish neighborhood in which they lived.

Because my grandfather was hospitalized when I was two years old in 1972 until his death in 1977 at the age of ninety, I never really had a chance to get to know him. However, his children and wife remember him fondly, describing him as gentle, kind, soft-spoken, and musical, yet one who stood firm on subjects such as strong religious observance and a good education. He always remained deeply hurt about the situation in Ireland and did not like to talk about it. Unlike the stereotypical view of the Irish immigrant, PJ did not frequent bars or like to drink. It is not surprising to learn that he was such a well-liked and respected man in his community and was often described as "very easy to get along with" by his peers.

The late Professor Raymond Kennedy of the Yale Department of Sociology once stated: "The history of the Irish people in America is one of our country's great true success stories. Coming here from an overcrowded and unproductive homeland, for the most part as poor and uneducated people, they have been quick to seize upon the opportunities their new homeland offered, and have risen to a commanding position in this, one of the most powerful nations in the world."[26] This statement directly applies to MaryKate and PJ. They came to this country with little more than a sixth-grade education, and raised four children who all have college degrees and have been successful in their lives. Jimmy and Peggy both became successful advertising executives in Manhattan; Theresa joined the Sisters of Charity in the early sixties, and has served as both a social worker for battered wives and a teacher. My father, William, is a high school AP European history and social studies teacher. All seven of MaryKate's grandchildren have college degrees as well, except for me, a college freshman.

PJ's family farm in Ulster is still owned by relatives, but the McCabe farm on which MaryKate grew up has long since switched hands. She is eighty-nine years old this April and is as quick as ever. I have never heard her complain about anything or get depressed when many other people would find things to gripe about. She is also one of the most sensible and sturdiest people I know. She also still has some of the old-world Irish in her. When we go to visit her, if a man gets up to make a cup of tea or something, she'll quickly turn to one of the granddaughters. "For Heaven's sake!" she'll exclaim, "Go and get your father a cup of tea!" She has led a hard but wonderful and rewarding life in which she found her solace in re-

Stephanie Courtney's paternal grandmother, MaryKate Courtney, in 1994.

ligion, and she still goes to church every day. What I find so wonderful is that her church, which is in view from the window of her Manhattan apartment she shares with her sister Margaret, is the same church in which she and PJ were married sixty-two years ago.

Note

1. As quoted in Francis J. Brown and Joseph Slabey Roucek, *One America: The History, Contributions, and Present Problems of Our Racial and National Minorities,* 3d ed. (Englewood Cliffs, N.J.: Prentice-Hall, 1952), 65.

Raffi Ishkanian (SUNY Binghamton 1994)

Roots Paper

It is said that in order to know where you are going, you have to know where you came from. Learning where ancestors came from, why they left, and how they adapted to life when they got here allows people to understand, in part, how they got to be who they are today.

Both of my father's parents immigrated to this country from Armenia in the early 1920s. Between the years 1915 and 1923, Turkish troops killed off 1.5 million Armenian men, women, and children. The Armenians had become victim to a Turkish nationalistic rhetoric similar to that of Nazi Germany. The genocide left this side of the family tree wanting for information, as contacts, information, and loved ones were lost during the flight for their lives.

My paternal grandmother, Takouhi Gulian, was born in the town Armenians knew as Caesaria, or what is today called by the Turks Kayseri. The town is located in the central portion of the Anatolian peninsula. She was born into a family of considerable standing within the community, as her father was a landowner as well as a judge. However, while she was still a young girl, both of her parents were slaughtered in the genocide. Takouhi was saved from the same fate by a local American Congregational Church mission benevolent enough to take her in. She was hidden from the Turks there and eventually transferred to another American Congregational Church mission near Istanbul. From the mission she received an education and, when she was old enough, passage to Philadelphia so that she might pursue schooling there, in order to become a nurse.

My paternal grandfather, Hagop Ishkanian, was born in the town Armenians knew as Sebastia, or what is today known by the Turks as Sivas. The town is located in the central portion of the Eastern Anatolian peninsula. His father was a poor, family farmer. With the advent of the Armenian genocide, Hagop and his brother John, fled their native land. The two fled Armenia through the Anatolian peninsula, hiding under the dead bodies of their countrymen by day and running by night. When they finally reached the Mediterranean Sea, they were rescued by some Greek fishermen and brought to safety in Greece. There, the two brothers worked and saved up enough money for the passage to America. At first, Hagop was rejected at Ellis Island because he had contracted pneumonia on the way over. He returned to Greece and had to start all over again.

Boston, New York City, and Fresno became the centers of Armenian immigration in the early years of the twentieth century. Hagop's second journey was successful, and he wound up settling in the Boston area. He found work at a shoe factory in Lynn, Massachusetts. My grandfather, along with many Armenians, had acquired shoemaking skills back in the Old Country, as it was customary there to make one's own shoes. He was fortunate in that most of his surviving family members settled in the same area.

Meanwhile, Takouhi's student visa had almost run out, so in order to keep her in the country, her older sister, living in Providence, Rhode Island, sought to find her a husband. She arranged for Hagop to come down to Providence to meet Takouhi. The two got along and saw each other about five times in the final year of her visa. Upon its expiration, the two were married in Montreal, Canada, with a local Armenian Oriental rug dealer serving as the best man.

They returned to Lynn, and from there moved to Ipswich, where a group of Armenians had invested in a shoe factory, in which all who worked owned a share. This effort failed during the Great Depression and Hagop lost much of his money, and with it his dream of becoming an auto mechanic. The two then moved to Providence, Rhode Island, where Hagop opened his own shoe repair shop. The business prospered and yet they moved again, this time back to Boston where they would remain the rest of their lives.

My father spent most of his adolescent years in the Boston neighborhood of Jamaica Plain. Although the neighborhood was decidedly Irish Catholic, the Ishkanian household never lost its Armenian ethnicity. The neighborhood was not an Armenian one, but Boston as a whole was, and still is, a mecca of the Armenian American community. Inside the Ishkanian house, Armenian was the only language spoken, and rarely was there ever a non-

Wedding portrait, Hagop and Takouhi Ishkanian, 1933.

Armenian inside it. They attended massive Armenian picnics, sometimes numbering over ten thousand people. They retained the food, the customs, and religion through an extensive communication network run predominantly with the church at its center. Takouhi did go to the local Congregational church regularly—as coincidence would have it, they had moved right across the street from one of the three Congregational churches that had sponsored the mission that had saved her life—but also made the long trip across town to the Armenian church whenever she could.

My father, Ara, thus was surrounded by the Armenian community his entire life. However, like most kids, he sought companionship with those who were most convenient. So as a result, most of his friends were Irish. His English developed rapidly, while Hagop's remained broken. Upon coming of age he considered changing his Armenian name from Ishkanian to Kanyan. However, his family never allowed him to lose knowledge of or contact with his Armenian identity. Because of this, when Ara went to college and began to search for himself, he began to gravitate more and more toward the Armenian community. He became president of the Boston University Armenian Club and an active member of the National Association of Armenian Studies and Research. He left his Irish friends behind for the Armenian social circles. He was now proud of his name and confident of who he was—an Armenian American.

Both of my mother's parents were born in Brooklyn. Both grew up in an ethnically German neighborhood. However, the ethnic experiences of the two are markedly different.

Frederick Cue, my maternal grandfather, is able to trace his roots in this country very far back. His mother, Emma Roedel, immigrated to New York City from Vienna, Austria. However, the Cue side of the family goes back considerably further. Frederick Cue's paternal great-grandfather William Cue immigrated to Philadelphia from Ireland at the turn of the nineteenth century. Although he emigrated from Ireland, he was of French Huguenot descent; his family is believed to have fled first from France to Ireland, and then to America.

My grandmother's father, Charles Asbeck, was born in Germany. He ran away from home at the age of sixteen because of an abusive stepmother and brother. He joined the merchant marines and jumped ship when his boat reached the harbors of New York in 1887. He enlisted in the army and fought in the Spanish-American War, in the process gaining his citizenship. My grandmother's mother immigrated to New York in 1870, also from Germany. The two married and settled in a railroad flat, crowded with the Asbeck extended family, in the Ridgewood section of Brooklyn.

Growing up, my grandfather was far more assimilated into American culture than was my grandmother. He lived in a German-speaking neighborhood and attended a German church and a weekly German school. However, with the advent of World War I, when it became unfashionable to maintain such habits, he stopped. German was spoken only at home in order to keep secrets from the kids. In 1925 the family moved from the ethnic Ridgewood section of Brooklyn to Hollis, Queens. Two years later, his parents separated.

My grandmother, on the other hand, was much more in touch with her ethnic identity growing up. She remained in Ridgewood until marriage. She continued to go to German school and church even during and after the First World War. Her family spoke German at home, and she was able to read and write the language as well. She became actively involved in the church and the German community that revolved around it. She continued to celebrate the major holidays in the German fashion.

Shortly after Frederick and Barbara married, the two moved up to East Greenbush, New York, just outside of Albany. My mother, Ellen, was born there in 1942. The move to the suburbs, coupled with the anti-German sentiment sparked by the Second World War, virtually eliminated any ethnicity in my mother's background. This fact would be a major reason behind her readiness to adopt the Armenian culture when she met my father.

According to *Webster's Dictionary,* to be ethnic is to be a member of a minority or nationality group that is part of a larger community. A major problem facing ethnic groups in America today is the need to maintain cohesiveness, while at the same time promoting success. It is easy for an ethnic group to remain networked and active when it is able to rely on the concentration of its people in ethnic neighborhoods. However, with the modern process of suburbanization, as members of ethnic groups succeed, they move out of the inner-city ethnic ghetto and into the suburb. In the more spread-out suburban environment it is much more difficult to maintain a cultural identity other than the norm. My mother's family offers a classic example of this phenomenon. Once out of the Ridgewood environment, it was very hard for the Cue family to maintain German customs. Where my grandmother and grandfather had had the luxury of being able to learn German from a school, my mother had to rely solely on the efforts of my grandparents. The German American community no longer dominated the ghettos; newcomers had diluted the ethnic population as German Americans died or moved away.

The Armenian American community is a lot younger than the German one, and perhaps that is one reason why it is much tighter today. Perhaps another reason is that it differs more from the mainstream European culture in that Armenia is in the Middle East and therefore frowned upon heavily by the American majority. Nevertheless, the Armenian American community is also experiencing the suburbanization problem.

Ethnicity has had a definite impact on my life. My mother, although an "odar" (Armenian for non-Armenian), has adopted the culture entirely, with a great deal of enthusiasm. She is active in the church choir (which sings only in Armenian), is part of an Armenian dance group, and has learned to cook most of the dishes. As a result, although I am genetically only half Armenian, I feel 100 percent Armenian. I attended the Armenian church and Armenian language school throughout my childhood. I live in the suburbs and did not have the benefit of having a lot of Armenians in my neighborhood. So like my father, I ended up with mostly non-Armenian friends. I always resented that I had to go to Armenian school on Fridays. My complaints found a deaf ear everywhere except amongst my Korean friends who had to go to Korean school and Korean church. I wanted to go to Catholic church. I hated that every time a substitute teacher would read off attendance and botch up my name, everyone was on the floor. I hated that whenever I got a trophy, my name was spelled wrong. I hated that whenever my name was in the paper for soccer, even when I got all-county honors, they spelled it wrong.

Yet, at the same time, I relished the tightness of my Armenian family. I loved how on holidays, and particularly Thanksgiving, we all got together. And as much as I hated that my church was different, I loved it. I loved the church picnics, the bazaars, the fact that almost all my parents' friends were there. I loved how it seemed like anywhere we went, if we found an Armenian, an instant friend was found. That ethnic bond was so strong. If we were in Canada, and ran into an Armenian, chances are we would find out that they were either a relative of a friend in church, or a good friend of so-and-so's in our church, or even from the same village back in Armenia. All I needed was people around me, in my immediate area, to appreciate it with me, to let me know it was okay to like these things that were so culturally different.

Like my father, in college I find myself liking more and more about my ethnicity and disliking less and less. I think that this is more than mere coincidence. The more education a person receives, the easier it becomes to see the value of one's ethnic identity. Children are uneducated as to the values of individuality. Childhood is one nonstop battle to fit in. Whether a kid is too smart, too slow, too unathletic, or too different, the kid is teased. In turn, the kid winds up hating that difference and perhaps education, combined with time, allows him or her to view that difference—that which makes him or her an individual—as an asset, rather than a handicap. I have become very proud of who I am. There are very few Armenians on this campus, yet rather than view that fact as a negative, I thrive on it. I jump at every chance I can get to talk about being Armenian, Armenia, or the genocide. It seems that today whenever an ethnic group gets together, the majority jumps on it as an excuse to say the group does not want to assimilate. These groups are needed because ethnicity is a vital part of a person's identity. For Armenians in particular, this struggle for recognition and distinction is vital. The genocide shattered the Armenian community into fragmented populations worldwide. The remembrance of these events, as for the victims of the Nazi Holocaust, is critical to the survival of the Armenian people. As long as my name is Raffi Ara Ishkanian, whether I want to be part of the Armenian ethnic community or not, my name will associate me with it, be it good or bad. And I am proud.

Bob Vaage (UC San Diego 1977)

A Family History

Who are we? Where are we from? How did we come to be in this place? I believe questions such as these need to be asked by all of us. However, we should not search for the answers just to satisfy our curiosity. Our history should be more than just a name in a book or a date from a forgotten past. It should be a basis for our future. For only when we know ourselves can we begin to understand others. We cannot know where we are going until we have seen where we have been.

My heritage has never been kept a secret from me. I have long been exposed to both sides of my family and the people and customs that make it up. The two sides of my family are as different as the North and South Poles, therefore making what I consider an interesting combination.

My father's roots seem to come straight out of the notes from one of our history lectures. He was born in 1925 in the small farming community of Newman Grove, Nebraska, to an Irish mother and a Norwegian father. His mother was the grandchild of an Irish immigrant who came to this country sometime during the potato famine. Her grandfather labored the rest of his life in New York. He did, however, save enough of his money to send his two sons to the Nebraska frontier following the Civil War. My grandfather Jacob Vaage was also a descendant of European immigrants. His grandparents came from a small farming community in southern Norway and settled in Minnesota. Two of their seven sons saw an opportunity to acquire new land, and following the Civil War they moved to the Nebraska frontier. There my grandfather was born, along with eight other brothers and sisters. In 1922 my Irish grandmother married an old Norwegian bachelor, my grandfather. In 1934 my grandfather lost his farm to the bank, and he and his family moved to California. From what I have seen, my grandmother's Irish heritage was buried upon her marriage to my grandfather. She was swallowed up in the Norwegian community. They raised their children in the Norwegian way. Although my grandmother never converted, her children were raised in the Lutheran Church. As for assimilation into American life, I don't believe it began for my father's family until his generation. Isolated in small farming towns in Minnesota and Nebraska, life remained much as it had been in the Old Country.

Long before Columbus reached the New World, several tribal groups made their homes in the Black Hills of what is now Wyoming and the Dakotas. It is to this origin that I can trace my mother's ancestors. The Shoshoni, Lakota, Yellow Hand, Crow, Blackfeet, and many smaller tribes lived in this area. For a thousand, perhaps two thousand, years these people were simple farmers and hunters. The arrival of white men in the New World changed their cultures greatly, even before they came into direct contact with them. In 1542 the Spanish conquistador Coronado swept north from Mexico in search of the seven cities of gold. Coronado remained less than a year, but he left something behind that was to change the natives' lives forever, the horse.

Through trading with tribes in the south, the people of the Black Hills obtained the horse. The tribes tamed and mastered the horse very swiftly, thereby obtaining the ability to follow the great buffalo herds down onto the plains of America. With the added mobility the horse gave them, tribes were separated by greater distances between the individual camps. In this manner came the formation of new tribes—among these the tribe that came to be known to the white man as the Comanche. Although they still spoke the same Shoshoni language, the Comanches had moved farther south of the main body of the Shoshoni over the course of one hundred years. The arrival of the white man in the 1800s pushed the Comanche even farther south into Arkansas, Oklahoma, Texas, and New Mexico. After nearly eighty years of war with the white man, and nearly two hundred with Mexicans, the Comanches signed a treaty at Medicine Lodge in 1867 and were placed on a reservation between the Red and Washita Rivers in southwest Oklahoma. Following eight years of starvation and bad treatment, the Comanches bolted the reservation and made one final stand with the Kiowas and Apaches in 1874. Following the massacre at Adobe Walls, they were returned to Oklahoma and were assigned to the Kiowa Reservation.

There are several different tribes within the Comanche tribe, including the Kwahadi, Penateka, Detsanayuka, Motsai, and Widyu. My mother is Kwahadi. My great-grandfather married my grandmother to a Spanish rancher whose family had been in New Mexico since its first settlement in the late sixteenth century. His reason for doing this was to allow my grandmother to escape the miseries of the reservation. They were married only ten years before he died. Their marriage produced only one child, my mother. Following my grandfather's death my grandmother moved to California instead of back to the reservation. After her graduation from UCLA with a teaching degree, my mother married my father in July 1944.

Being kept practically in solitary confinement on the prisons known as reservations, the Kwahadi Comanche, as well as most other American tribes, are in my view probably the least assimilated of all groups of people in this country.

Stemming from my family background I've been exposed to an interesting cross section of the people of this country: from the farm towns of Middle America, to the ghettos of South Central and East Los Angeles where my mother has taught, to the reservations of New Mexico and Oklahoma, to suburbia. I feel a growing sense of identity and pride among people today. I am disappointed in those of my generation who have gained the education and insight, yet failed to respond to the needs of society. It seems that many people are still chained by the same fears that arrived with the first white men to settle this country.

The Great King told me the path should never be crooked, but open to everyone to pass and repass. As we all live in one land, I hope we shall love as one people.

Little Carpenter

Susan Carnicelli (SUNY Binghamton 1990)

My Austrian-Italian Ethnicity

All four of my grandparents immigrated to the United States from Europe prior to World War II. My maternal grandparents, Erna Herzog and Eric Vogel, were born in Vienna, Austria, at the turn of the century. They married in 1934 and continued living in Vienna with no intentions of leaving. My grandfather worked as a self-employed plumber while my grandmother worked in Gerngross, a department store in the heart of Vienna. Since my grandparents were Jewish, they began to realize the dangers of staying in Austria with the rise of Hitler in the mid-1930s. But even though they were Jewish and saw a need to leave, it took a great deal of convincing from my grandmother to uproot my grandfather from Viennese culture. In fact, my grandmother often told my mother how she had to threaten my grandfather with divorce in order to get him to leave. Finally in September of 1939 my grandparents, who were among the very last Jews to escape from Vienna, left their mothers behind and traveled to France. At this point the war had begun, so a warship escorted their passenger ship to Manhattan. At the time, neither of my grandparents could speak English, and for the first three weeks in New York they lived at the H.I.A.S.—the Hebrew Immigrant Aid Society. My grandfather's brother had left Vienna several years earlier. He was one of few who obtained a visa directly from the Dachau concentration camp, where he had been placed for being a socialist. Since my great-uncle was already settled in New York, he welcomed my grandparents to live with them for a few months.

Eventually they found jobs, my grandfather as a plumber and my grandmother as a seamstress. Shortly after, they found an apartment in Prospect Heights, Brooklyn. Slowly they began to learn English, mostly from the radio. In addition, my grandfather began to learn Yiddish at work although my grandmother never caught on.

Although my grandparents lived in a Jewish neighborhood, these people were all American-born, with ancestors primarily from Russia and Poland. In my grandparents' household only German was spoken. So when my mother was born in 1943, she learned German as her first language. My grandmother once told my mother that her Jewish American friends in Brooklyn often warned my grandparents not to speak German on the street because people would think they were the "enemy." My grandparents often were nervous in public, and did not speak to each other at all until they returned to their apartment. So I am sure, although my grandparents lived among friends, they felt much discomfort in America. They saw themselves as Austrians and were devastated that they had to leave due to their religion.

After a few years of living in the United States, my grandfather decided to search for other Austrian immigrants. He became founder and president of the Vienna Club. This was a purely social organization with approximately sixty members. Each year they held gatherings, dances, and New Year's Eve parties. This gave my grandparents an outlet of Austrian Jewish friends. They reminisced about old times and indulged in delicious Viennese cuisine, often prepared by my grandmother.

Another outlet for my grandparents was the Catskills. Each summer my grandparents and my mother spent a month in Fleischmanns and Pinehill, New York. Here Austrian, German, and Hungarian Jews gathered in resorts, speaking only German and reliving their European days.

Since my mother was always involved in these cultural gatherings, she was constantly reminded that her culture was that of the Vienna of Freud, Mahler, and the Hapsburg Empire. But her neighborhood in Brooklyn was not ethnically similar to her own background. These differences in ethnicity and class status caused my mother to feel slightly detached in her youth. Over time her uneasiness disappeared.

My paternal grandparents also immigrated to the United States during the same era, but their reasons for coming to America were quite different. My father's father, Anthony Carnicelli, and my father's mother, Julia Romanelli, were born in Agropola in the province of Salerno, Italy. This area is rich in history. It is known as the Siren Land of antiquity, and my grand-

Eric and Erna Vogel with their daughter, Joan, Brooklyn, 1944.

parents' town is only five or six miles from the magnificent Greek temples of Paesturn, located at one of the principal sites of the Greek colony in Italy known as the Magna Graecia. My grandfather came from a poor but distinguished family that could trace its history back to the thirteenth century, and my grandmother was the only surviving child of a minor government official. Throughout her life, she considered herself socially "superior" to my grandfather because of her middle-class status.

In 1921, at the age of fourteen, my grandfather came to the United States with his father, who was in the merchant marines. He worked on a dock in Manhattan and traveled back and forth to Italy. At the age of twenty-three, he returned to Italy to marry his childhood sweetheart.

It was my grandfather who wanted to settle in America, mostly for economic reasons. He saw more promise in Manhattan than in Italy. So in August 1930 my grandparents immigrated by ship to the United States. Like my maternal grandparents they lived with relatives for a short while in Borough Park, Brooklyn. My grandmother soon gave birth to my father in 1931, while my grandfather worked as a shoemaker.

When I speak to my grandmother now, she tells me that she would much rather have remained in Italy, since at the time America was faced with the hardships of the Great Depression. Work was not as profitable as my grandfather had expected it to be, yet he still had no nostalgic illusions about Italy, which for him represented only economic hardship and political oppression. He also detested the Fascist regime, which was then in power. After the birth of my father in 1931 my grandmother became more settled and content with American life. Although they stayed, economic hardships forced my grandmother to get a job as a seamstress at extremely low wages.

My grandmother still lives in Brooklyn, and tells me she did not feel any nativist criticism upon arrival in New York. I believe, however, this was so only because she lived (and still lives) in an Italian immigrant neighborhood where the majority of her friends and coworkers shared the same ethnicity. This isolation probably closed her off from the rest of American society where nativist sentiment was more common.

My father is now a professor of English at the City University of New York, and it is ironic that his first language, like my mother's, was not English. As a young child he spoke only Italian, and it was not until kindergarten that he began to learn English. In first grade, when his teacher told the class to make glue with flour and water, he could not understand how to take an actual *flower* and manufacture glue from it. Despite these trivial problems, he quickly caught on and spoke English well among his Ital-

Julia Carnicelli and her son, Domenick, Brooklyn, 1932.

ian friends. It was not until high school that he felt different and uncomfortable. In elementary school his fellow students were all of Italian descent, but at Fort Hamilton High School the majority of the students were Irish and Scandinavian. These students did not treat my father any differently, but he felt physically different. His small group of Italian friends for the most part did not take education seriously, but my father worked hard and received good grades. This experience made my father realize the diversity of American culture.

In Brooklyn my father was raised Roman Catholic, and he attended church regularly. But though he was devout, he had great religious and temperamental differences with the Roman Catholic clergy. At the age of sixteen his differences with the church were so great that, for all practical purposes, he broke all connections.

Both of my parents became the first members of their families to graduate from college. My father received his M.A. from Brooklyn College and went on to Columbia University to receive his Ph.D. During his graduate work, he taught at Brooklyn College where he met my mother. Despite their different ethnic and religious backgrounds they got along well.

When my parents decided to marry, it became a touchy issue. At first my maternal grandparents objected, fearing a revival of anti-Semitic feelings like those in Europe, and were concerned for the well-being of my mother. Despite this opposition, my parents married in 1964, and after living in Brooklyn for eight years, settled in New Rochelle, New York. Even though my grandparents were different ethnically, they got along remarkably well. I can remember both of my grandmothers sitting around my kitchen table comparing immigration stories, discussing their similar jobs, and trying to outdo each other with poverty stories. Over the years they grew extremely close.

As far as my ethnicity goes, I have always been aware of my Austrian-Italian background. Both of my parents have always described and discussed their parents' experiences as well as their own stories. In addition, I have always taken part in ethnic and cultural traditions. Italian and Austrian cuisine have enhanced my ethnic awareness. What I find most interesting is others' responses to my heritage.

Since my father objected to many aspects of the Catholic church in his youth, my older brother and I have followed our mother's religion. We attended Hebrew school and were Bar and Bas Mitzvahed. Throughout elementary, middle, and high school, my peers have had trouble understanding my ethnicity. When I explain to people that I am an American, of Austrian-Italian descent, and of the Jewish religion, they automatically label me an Italian Jew, disregarding my Austrian background. I have observed that people have classified Jews as an ethnic group instead of a religious group. People fail to realize that there are Russian Jews, Polish Jews, Hungarian Jews, Italian Jews, Czech Jews, and so on. Instead of seeing Judaism as a religion, many people falsely view it as a nationality.

In addition, since I have the surname Carnicelli, anti-Semites, unaware of my religion, feel free to voice their bigotry against Jews. Ironically, those who know I'm Jewish often say cruel things about Italians and Catholics. The vicious, senseless comments that I have heard have opened my eyes to the feelings of isolation many immigrants must have felt when they arrived in this country.

In reconsidering my ethnic origins, I must admire my grandparents' courage. Their ability to immigrate to a country without the ability to speak the language is an accomplishment in itself. Although they did not leave and enter under the best conditions, I feel they made the best of American life and for the most part integrated well. Through my own experiences, I see that the confusion of ethnic and religious origins must be a common occurrence in American culture, due to the increasing tendency for ethnic and religious groups to intermix. Hopefully in the future people will judge each other by personality, not by name, ethnic background, or religion.

Josephine Burgos (SUNY Binghamton 1994)

East Side Story: What *West Side Story* Left Out

Puerto Rico—my heart's devotion.
Let it sink back into the ocean.
Always the hurricanes blowing.
Always the population growing.
. . .
I like the island Manhattan!

These are the first few lines of the famous song "America" from the American movie *West Side Story.* All my life these words have haunted me. It seems that for as long as I can remember whenever I told a non-Hispanic that I was a Puerto Rican, this movie has been brought up. It is a popular opinion among many Americans that the representation of Puerto Ricans in *West Side Story* was accurate. Many of these people forget that this movie was a musical written by whites in an effort to rehash Shakespeare's *Romeo and Juliet.* Since the release of this film, Puerto Ricans have been battling the belief that we hate our island and that our lives in New York have been nothing but a song and a dance. Yes, life in Puerto Rico is very hard, but the lives of Puerto Rican migrants in America have been just as difficult. The things that Anita says in the song "America" have very rarely been the opinion of the average Puerto Rican living in New York. Most Puerto Ricans who live in the states love our island and visit it as often as they can. Oh, and by the way, Natalie Wood, the actress who played Maria, is NOT a Puerto Rican. Now that that has been said let us show the actual experience behind *West Side Story.*

My maternal grandmother, Maria Concepcion DeJesus, was born in Rio Piedras, Puerto Rico in 1914. Although she could read and write, she never received more than an elementary education. Concepcion, one of nine children, had to quit school early in life to go to work and help support her family. When she was only thirteen years old she got a job sewing tobacco that was hung on lines to dry. This was very hard work, but she had to do it to help keep her family afloat. In fact, as soon as she received her paycheck she, like her sisters, had to give it to her father. One time Concepcion actually opened up her paycheck and bought herself a pair of knee-highs before she went home. When her father found out what she had done he gave her a horrible beating because this was unacceptable behavior. When you got paid you were supposed to give the money to your parents and that was all there was to it.

In 1930, at the age of sixteen, Concepcion married Jose Rodriguez. Some time after her marriage, Concepcion's sister Rosa moved to New York City. Through the help of a friend, Rosa found a job and an apartment and wrote Concepcion that she should migrate to New York also. Because she was having marital difficulties, Concepcion flew to join her sister in 1943, but due to the lack of funds she was forced to leave her three children behind with their father. It was very difficult for her to do this, but she did what she felt was necessary.

Once Concepcion arrived in New York she lived with her sister Rosa in what is now known as Spanish Harlem. This is on the Upper East Side of Manhattan. She quickly found a job as a seamstress in a factory and saved all her money for an entire year to buy the airline tickets for her children to come to New York. A year after her arrival, Concepcion sent three airline tickets and three big pink ribbons to her children. Her daughters, Sylvia (age 12) and Frances (age 3), were supposed to wear the ribbons in their hair, while her son, Andrew (age 8), was to wear his ribbon around his neck. Concepcion believed that these ribbons would enable her to pick the children out of a crowd once they arrived at the airport. Fate, however, had other plans.

The plane ride was terribly frightening for the children, who were flying without a companion and could speak no English. Also, as luck would have it, many passengers began to panic because there was a great deal of turbulence. This only served to frighten the children more, but the real nightmare began after their airplane landed. The children's flight was scheduled to land at Idlewild Airport (now Kennedy Airport), but due to congestion was redirected to La Guardia Airport. The children, therefore, found themselves lost and alone in a strange city and knew that their mother might not be able to find them. Luckily, a very nice gentleman, who could speak Spanish, saw the children crying in a corner and asked if he could help them. Once Sylvia, the eldest, apprised him of their situation this good Samaritan hailed a taxi and took them to Idlewild Airport. Unfortunately, when they reached Idlewild the information desk clerk told them that everybody waiting for their flight had already been sent to La

Concepcion DeJesus on her farm in Rio Piedras, Puerto Rico, ca. 1984.

Josephine Burgos's mother, Frances, at about two years old, in Puerto Rico.

Guardia Airport and that they had probably just missed their mother. Seeing the children's growing distress, this gentleman bought them lunch and then took them back to La Guardia Airport. This time when the taxi reached its destination the children spotted their mother and eagerly tumbled out of the car to greet her. After a tear-filled reunion, Sylvia told Concepcion about their adventure. When she turned to introduce her mother to their savior, however, the stranger was gone. To this day my family does not know who this man was, but we are all grateful to him. Without his intervention who knows what would have happened to my Aunt Sylvia, my Uncle Andrew, and my mother, Frances.

After Concepcion was reunited with her children, she struggled to earn enough money to get her own apartment. The factory she worked for employed mostly Puerto Rican women to sew plastic covers for pillows, mattresses, and sofas. The conditions in the factory were miserable. Employees had only one half-hour break during the entire day and they had to work on Saturdays. They had to work in silence, and the boss would walk around to see what they were doing. As soon as a seamstress finished a batch she had to call out to get another batch. Their hands were moving constantly. Sometimes a seamstress's hand would get caught under the needle of her machine, but she still had to keep working. She would only be given enough time to bandage her hand, and then she had to get right back to work. In the factory, employees were paid by the piece, so they had to do a lot of work just to earn a little money. In the summer it often got very hot, especially since they were working with plastic. Some workers could afford to buy fans, but the ones that couldn't just had to suffer. Factory owners didn't invest much money to get things fixed either. Sanitation was horrible and there was very poor lighting. Concepcion hated the film *West Side Story* because the factory in that movie was nothing like the real factories. Maria and Anita's factory was very clean, while real factories were horrible sweatshops. And you better believe that real-life seamstresses didn't have any time to be singing.

Because she couldn't speak English, Concepcion had to stick with the Hispanic community at first. She battled with the language, but eventually picked it up at work and by defending herself while she was shopping. Eventually Concepcion moved from Spanish Harlem to the Lower East Side of Manhattan. At the time that area was predominantly Italian and Eastern European, so she had to learn English in order to survive. She even managed to teach herself how to read and write in English.

When the children were still in Puerto Rico, the burden was on Sylvia to take care of her brother and sister. Even though they lived with their father, she was their primary caretaker. When they left Puerto Rico, their father was sad to see them go, but it was his belief that children belonged with their mother. In New York, Concepcion enrolled Sylvia and Andrew in public school, while she left the baby, Frances, with neighbors. Once school let out, Sylvia had her brother and sister under her charge.

When Concepcion could finally afford to, she took her children out of the public school system and put them in Catholic school, because she felt that they would receive a better education there. Nevertheless, all three children had a very difficult time in school. At that time bilingual education didn't really exist, so the children found themselves being left back year after year. In fact, Sylvia and Andrew never made it past the sixth and seventh grades.

During the late 1940s Concepcion met Augosto Trippichio, who soon became her common-law husband. In 1950 Concepcion gave birth to their daughter, Gladys. Concepcion's salary was the family's only source of income. After a great deal of struggle she finally had to accept that with a new baby in the house some sacrifices had to be made. She could no longer afford to put three children through private school and hire baby-sitters for Gladys. She, therefore, had to take Sylvia and Andrew out of school. Andrew had to work in a leather factory to help support the family, while Sylvia stayed home with the baby. Concepcion valued education and hated to rob her children of one, but she could find no other alternative. Frances and Gladys, however, did finish high school, much to their mother's joy.

After high school, Frances worked as a sales clerk at J&G's Sporting Goods store. Aside from cashier work, Frances had to sew lettering on shirts, jerseys, and jackets, and stuff boxing gloves. At that time boxing gloves had to be stuffed with horse hair, which can harm a person's health if inhaled. Unfortunately, this store was poorly ventilated and the clerks were never provided with masks to cover their noses. Many of these clerks, including Frances, got sick. Frances went to secretarial school at night, however, and eventually found an office job with the Board of Education. Until she got married, Frances, like her mother before her, had to give the majority of her wages to her mother to help support the family.

My father, Jose Manuel Burgos, was born in Arecibo, Puerto Rico, in 1936. Like Concepcion, Jose received only an elementary education and had to leave school to help support his family. There were six children in Jose's family and he was the second oldest. His older brother, Adrian, had already left the family to settle in New York City, so a great deal of the financial responsibilities fell on Jose's shoulders.

It was very difficult to find work in Puerto Rico, so Jose became a migrant worker with his father. At the age of eighteen he joined a migrant workers' group that picked beans on upstate New York farms. At the bean farm the men had to get up before sunrise to go to work in the fields. They spent long hours doing backbreaking work and didn't leave the fields until after dark. On the farm there was an overseer, who told the workers what to do simply by pointing at things and making signals. None of the farm owners ever even bothered to learn Spanish to communicate with the workers. The workers were given food and shelter, but both left something to be desired. On the farm there was a big barn that had rows of cots in it. This is where the workers slept and they very rarely had much to protect themselves from the cold.

In 1955, at the end of the picking season, Jose decided that he didn't want to return to Puerto Rico with his father and the rest of the workers. He wanted to join his brother and try his luck in New York City. Unfortunately, however, he didn't speak any English. All he had was a piece of paper with his brother's address on it. Jose kept showing this address to people and through sign language they told him what buses to take. Luckily he made it to his brother's apartment without too many mishaps. It's a miracle that he isn't still wandering around bus stations today.

Jose stayed with his brother Adrian until he could find his own place. This was on Amsterdam Avenue in Manhattan, which was a popular Hispanic neighborhood at the time. Jose finally rented a room in a building where the bathroom in the hall was shared by all the tenants. Then, when he was in his early twenties, Jose moved in with a Puerto Rican woman who was a nurse. By 1959 they had a daughter named Theresa.

At first, Jose got a job in a lamp factory, but he still didn't know any English. In fact, one day he had a really bad stomachache, but didn't know how to tell his boss. He only knew the word headache so he kept saying the word headache and pointed at his stomach. It took quite a while for them to figure out what he was trying to say, and when they did they made a lot of fun of him, but they did let him go home. The conditions in the factory at this time were very similar to those that Concepcion experienced, but they were somewhat more lenient. When Concepcion was first working in the factory, there was no way that her boss would have let her go home because of a stomachache. Eventually, though, Jose did get a job outside of the dreaded factories. He became a truck driver and delivered groceries for a supermarket called Gristedes.

Much like Concepcion, Jose taught himself English because it was necessary to survive. Those who didn't learn English had no chance of getting out of the factories. Jose taught himself English by reading the sports section of the local newspapers. He loved boxing and the New York Mets, so he would buy both the English newspapers and the Spanish newspapers, *El Diario* or *La Prensa.* (*El Diario* is still being published today.) First Jose would read the Spanish paper and then would read the English newspapers to see if they said the same thing. Jose was always determined to know what was going on in the sports world, especially for the New York Mets. It was this determination that drove him to learn how to read English.

Jose was always very aware of American prejudices against Puerto Ricans. He talked a great deal about how Puerto Ricans were treated in American society. For example, he was often enraged by the fact that Puerto Ricans were always blamed for crimes committed by other Hispanics. The American media never had anything nice to say about Puerto Rico or Puerto Ricans. That hurt people like Jose and Concepcion and her children a lot, but at times they had to force themselves to ignore it. Also, there was an awful lot of discrimination against Puerto Ricans in both the workforce and the education system. Jose and the others were all touched by this quite often.

In August 1966 Jose met Frances at a dance. Contrary to what *West Side Story* might have us believe, dances were very segregated in New York. White people had their dances, while Hispanics had dances with salsa and merenge music. The two groups did not mix.

In June 1967 Jose and Frances were married at Mary Help of Christians Church. Jose was thirty; Frances was twenty-five. By September 1967 they were given custody of Jose's daughter, Theresa. The couple raised the girl for three years, at which point she went back to live with her mother. I was born two years later in March 1972.

Both of my parents worked hard and suffered a lot throughout their lives. They tried to make me as Americanized as possible because they wanted to see me succeed. They were afraid that if I was raised in a bilingual household I would have a hard time assimilating to American society. They always taught me to love and respect my culture and heritage, but they also taught me that you had to be as American as possible if you wanted to make it in this country. They struggled to shelter me from the racism and prejudice that they themselves had experienced. Despite their efforts, however, I was touched time and again by those same prejudices. I still remember my first day in the first grade. The school's principal came into our classroom and looked down at the class roster. She took every student that had a Latin American last name and put us in an English as a Second Language (ESL) class. She never even gave us a test to see if we be-

Josephine Burgos and her mother at Josephine's first birthday party, Brooklyn, 1973.

longed there. She just automatically assumed that we couldn't speak English and made us stay in that class for the whole year. I have been offended in many other similar ways throughout my twenty-two years in this country, and I expect many more affronts to occur. I must admit that if there was anything accurate in *West Side Story,* it was the hatred shown by the white characters toward the Puerto Ricans.

My parents divorced when I was seven and I am estranged from my father. My mother has gone on to finish her bachelor's degree and is currently working on a master's. Since I can remember she has worked during the day, seen to my needs in the afternoon, and gone to college at night. Together she and I have tried to honor the struggles of my grandmother and father as immigrants in New York and to show the world that we Puerto Ricans feel nothing but love for our beautiful lone-star in the Caribbean.

> I close my eyes. I am in paradise.
> Say you'll be there, my Puerto Rico.
> Hold me tonight under the stars.
> Puerto Rico!
> . . . .
> I'm coming home to you!
>
> "Puerto Rico" from the movie *Salsa*

Gloria Genel (UC San Diego 1988)

Three Generations in America

In coming from Mexico to the United States, "the great land of opportunity," my maternal grandmother sought a better way of life for herself and her young daughter. To obtain this economic stability, however, she soon realized there was a price they had to pay, and this was that they must learn to adapt and acculturate themselves to this new and foreign environment. This meant having to adjust to the standards of a distinct dominating society. As they were very much aware and proud of their identities, they held onto their cultural heritage. Looking over several generations, we can see both adaptation and assimilation to the American way of life and yet at the same time a preservation and retaining of many Mexican cultural traits. My grandmother was clearly enticed by the many opportunities that America had to offer and became the first person in my family to immigrate to the United States. For this reason I base this essay primarily on her experiences and those of succeeding generations.

In the late 1940s Bartola Martinez did something that would drastically change her future and that of her descendants: she left her hometown of Guadalajara, Mexico. Forty years old and an unwed mother with a three-year-old daughter, she packed what few belongings she owned, boarded a bus, and set off for her new destination—Mexicali, Mexico, a town that borders the United States. Like many other immigrants, Bartola was pushed to leave the interior of Mexico primarily because of her gradually deteriorating economic situation. Unable to find work in Guadalajara and running out of money quickly, she needed to find a new source of income.

Relatives who had settled some time before in Mexicali had kept in touch with Bartola, and through letters described to her how easy it was to find jobs in the area and how inexpensive everything was. These motives influenced her to travel to this border town.

So Bartola, along with her daughter, Maria, settled in Mexicali. All went well for them for a period of about eight years, until in the mid-1950s once again Bartola was faced with a dry spell in employment. This time, however, in searching for a job she ventured to go further than she had gone before, beyond the border to the United States. The pull factor that she experienced in coming to America was basically that she needed work and had heard of the many opportunities available in the land of plenty. She entered the country illegally at first, but later on became a citizen. As she recalls, it was quite easy to walk across the border without being hassled by the immigration officials. In El Centro, California, a city about ten miles from the border, she began her new life.

It was with the help of relatives and friends, as before, that she found work as a domestic helper with several families. Mexican women in this period were commonly employed as domestics or nannies with Anglo-American families. Bartola worked with two different families before she came to work for Tom and Wylma Zoslocki and their three small children, John, Mike, and Billy. Before anything else, the Zoslocki's shortened and somewhat changed Bartola's name to something easy that they could all pronounce; she would from then on be known as Lola.

At the time she was hired, it was not clear to anyone the importance that this small, gray-haired lady would play in the family. Lola's ambivalence about assimilating or acculturating is most clearly seen soon after this. She obviously functioned well and became an integral part of this Anglo family while still preserving her cultural values. Yet instead of her gradually changing herself to suit their needs, they began to change for her. Rather than always cooking typical American foods and dishes for the family, Lola would cook what she knew how to, and that was generally Mexican food. The language issue is another example of her refusal to adapt completely. She could not, or perhaps more correctly, would not, learn the English language. She believed that it was too difficult for her and felt it would be useless to her since she planned eventually to return to Mexico anyway. The Zoslockis instead began learning Spanish bit by bit. Slowly they were able to communicate with Lola, and it seems unusual that the entire family would conform to the native language of this one woman. Perhaps another reason why she refused to learn English is because of the proximity of El Centro to Mexico. Since the border was so close, there were many Spanish speakers everywhere, so that she didn't necessarily have to learn English to communicate with others in that area.

Lola became very attached to the Zoslocki children, in particular to the youngest, three-year-old Billy. Since their mother was always at work or out somewhere Lola became, according to the children, their "second mother." The bond between these two has been so strong that it survived all cultural, language, and economic barriers. Today, Billy is a well-established businessman with a family of his own, but in Lola's eyes he will always be her little boy. Billy also has not forgotten Mama Lola, and even though the one true barrier that separates them now is geographical distance, he visits her at least several times a year, as does the rest of the Zoslocki family. To many individuals, working for so many years as a domestic would appear to be a stagnant, degrading position, but for Lola it turned out to be a very fortunate experience.

Lola's daughter, Maria, did not come to the United States with her mother at first. Instead she stayed in Mexicali and was cared for by her uncle and his wife for approximately a year while her mother worked in the United States. It was not until the couple decided to return to Guadalajara that Lola was presented with what she considered to be a very serious problem: who was to look after her daughter? There was no one else she could leave Maria with and she was afraid to ask her employers for permission to bring her daughter to live with her for fear of losing her job. Eventually faced with no other solution, she confronted the Zoslockis with her problem. Contrary to the reactions she had expected, both Tom and Wylma were happy to be able to help her. Soon after, Lola returned to Mexico for Maria and brought her to the United States.

Twelve-year-old Maria came to the United States not knowing how to speak a word of English. Being still a child, however, made it much easier for her to assimilate than it had been for her mother, who had merely adapted to her new environment. Almost immediately after arriving in the United States she began junior high school. At first, the group of children that she interacted with was primarily composed of other Hispanic children who spoke Spanish. As soon as she began to learn the language, however, she started to branch out and socialized with others outside her group. Although there was a sudden change in her surroundings, she quickly learned the language and began to adjust to the different standards of her new country. Just as her mother had, Maria also became very attached to the Zoslocki family. Over a period of years she grew to be not only Lola's daughter but also a daughter of Tom and Wylma, and an older sister to the boys.

In 1966, after working for the Zoslockis for about ten years, Lola, now feeling old and weary, decided to retire and return to Mexico. Maria had to make a choice of either staying in the United States or going back to Mexico with her mother. It was a tough decision, but having only each other and being very close to her mother made her choose to return to Mexico. After adjusting so well to the American way of life, the sudden change in environment was more drastic than she had expected. In the United States, Maria had been very much aware of her identity and held onto her Mexican culture. Returning to Mexico once again made her realize how American she really was; she felt like a stranger in the land of her birth. At this point in her life Maria realized she was no longer strictly Mexican. She longed so much for the life she had once led in the United States. In April 1967 Maria married her childhood sweetheart from Mexicali, Alfred M. Genel. Shortly after her marriage she returned to the United States once more, apparently realizing that no matter how much she valued and clung to her Mexican heritage and culture, she also valued the newly discovered American side of herself. The young couple—my parents—moved just across the border to the California town of El Centro.

In 1968 I was born, the first of three children; later on would come my sister, Patricia, and my brother, Freddy. Ever since I can remember I, like my mother and grandmother, have been proud of my identity. My ethnicity plays a very important part in my life. It defines who I am and the role that I play in American society. I believe that I am much more assimilated than my grandmother or mother, but I still retain much of the Mexican culture that has been passed down through each generation. I feel that my generation is not strictly Mexican or American but an equal mixture of both, a combination containing the best of these two worlds. I will never abandon my cultural heritage but rather will encourage my children and grandchildren to find pride in who they are and continue to share my values just as I share those of my grandmother.

Catholicism is one of the connections that links the three generations of women in my family. It was my grandmother's strong religious beliefs that kept her going throughout her life. Many times she felt tired and wanted to give up her struggle against life in general, but to this day she says, "God always managed to give me strength," and so she never gave in but picked herself up once again and kept on going. Similarly, my mother also held religion as an important part of her life. Overwhelmed with the many problems encountered in marriage and the upbringing of three children, her faith in God continues to persist. My life without the Catholic religion would be quite unfulfilled. Just as it was important in the

Three generations of the Genel family, Lola, Maria, and Gloria, 1993.

lives of my grandmother and mother, it also plays a major role in every aspect of my life. Consequently, even though the focus of Catholicism itself may have shifted somewhat over the three generations, its importance in our lives was not changed or lost in any way.

Another important element that has been conserved and passed down from the generations before me is the significance of family and togetherness. Unity within the family and the community is of utmost importance and plays a major role in our lives as well as that of other Mexican Americans. This was especially true in the case of my mother and grandmother. Since it was only the two of them, each of them represented everything that the other had, so they tried never to be separated. After my mother married and returned to the United States, my grandma Lola could not bear to be away from her only child and soon after left Mexico for the United States. Even though being in Mexico was important, and coming to this country meant having to adjust once more, it was a small price to pay for being near her daughter.

In comparing the three generations of women in my family, I have become quite aware of the assimilation process. From my grandmother who chose to adapt rather than assimilate, to my mother who was somewhat more assimilated, and then to me there is a gradual pattern of increasing assimilation. As individuals, we are very distinct in some ways, but at the same time we share many things in common. There are certain values, morals, and beliefs within us that time itself has not destroyed; rather, they have helped strengthen the ties between generations. All of these things that have been passed on have helped shape me to be the person I am today. They have made me proud to be who I am and not deny my ethnicity or my roots, and I will do my best to share these values with succeeding generations.

LaToya Powell (SUNY Binghamton 1994)

Where I Stand and Why

Although generations before me did not come to the United States from a different country, we as African Americans have endured our own form of immigration. My family, originally from Lumberton, North Carolina, migrated to New York City in the fall of 1957. My grandfather Franklin Powell left North Carolina at the age of twenty-three with his eighteen-year-old wife, Shirley Ruth Powell, in search of a decent job and a better life for his new family.

I interviewed my grandfather to find out what similarities I saw between us, drawing on the concepts of bordercrossing and traveling. The concepts of bordercrossing and traveling entail not only the idea of moving from one space to another but also the idea of encountering the unknown. From certain standpoints, bell hooks states, "To travel is to encounter the terrorizing force of white supremacy."[1] It is with this encounter that my grandfather was forced to adopt certain ideas and values that he instilled in his children. Since he and my grandmother are the only parents I've known, their ideas made me the person I am today, and the decisions he made for his family reflect upon the woman I will become.

I started out by asking my grandfather, "To what degree did our family feel it was necessary to adapt to white America in the South?" He replied by saying, "We had no choice but to adapt to white America because they had all of the work; they were our main source of survival. The young men worked from day to day, nothing was permanent. And your grandmother worked cleaning houses for the whites that lived nearby." I went on to ask my grandfather, "How did you feel about voting, jobs, and Jim Crow laws? Did you live in a predominantly white or black neighborhood?" He replied, "Jim Crow laws affected me in every aspect of public service. I was young and did not question why these laws were implemented. I would only hear my mother and the elders of the town complain; the teenagers did not notice. All we knew was that there was a white, black, and Indian bathroom; we never asked why we couldn't all use the same one." My grandfather also told me that jobs in the South were scarce, especially after the tobacco season had ended and the harvesting was done. He also sharecropped for the whites and picked their cotton. Once this was finished, times got harder than they already were.

I asked my grandfather, "How did education rank in your list of priorities?" He went on to tell me that education was not a main concern in his life. He was very young and admitted that he did not look very far into the future. His only concern was work and the survival of his family. Once my grandfather came to New York City, he concentrated on getting a good job, and this he did accomplish. He worked for the New York City Transit Authority for the next thirty years of his life and is now retired. During this time he brought into the world and raised five children—six including myself—and in this time he constantly stressed the importance for survival in this white corporate world. He explained to me that he left North Carolina with only a sixth-grade education and was fortunate to receive such a good job. I was raised with only the best and was sent to the best school he could find in our small, predominantly white neighborhood. He felt that if I went to the best schools and had everything the white children around me had, it would make it easier for me to succeed. After a large number of African Americans moved into my neighborhood, all of the whites left. I now had black friends, I went to an all-black school, and I spoke Black English. Of all of the changes that had occurred, my speaking Black English annoyed him the most. Sending me to a predominantly white university enforced his conformist ideas. It also forced me to take on two separate identities.

The bus ride home is just enough time for me to complete my transformation process. When I'm in Binghamton, things are different: my guard is down, there's a smile on my face, and I am somewhat carefree. Once I step off of the bus at Port Authority Bus Terminal, I'm a changed person: no time for smiling, only time for attitude. The same way I reform in character, my language takes a turn. I am no longer this standard-English-speaking college girl; I'm a Black-English-speaking city girl.

I never thought that college in any way affected my identity at home.

From my perspective, I used to think it was all the same person; my aunt was the one who slapped me with this rude awakening; she said I sound white. "Educated" was the first thing that came to my mind; because I wasn't speaking slang or Black English, that made me white. To my grandfather, who never had a formal education, this is wonderful. He is proud of the fact that I don't speak Black English. As far as he is concerned, Black English does not exist—it is not a language. English is very important to him; he walks around the house correcting everyone saying, "How hard is it to take a few seconds more and think about what you're saying? It takes no more breath to say it correctly." The only reason he feels this way is because if I can hold a conversation with corporate white folk it will mean that I have succeeded—I've overcome, I've finally made it—at least in his eyes. This degree of success is enough for him because, as I said, he didn't receive formal education and he was lucky to get a good-paying job for thirty years and live comfortably during this time. You cannot do this anymore. A lot of his feelings stem from his love and wanting his granddaughter to have more in life, but a lot of it reflects a conformist ideology. If we conform, then we will fit in. It is a cause and effect situation. If I learn to speak standard English, the effect will be my survival in this world.

Black English is my foundation, and it gives me the strength to return to school and deal with the crowd that believes that my only choice is to assimilate. Gloria Anzaldúa describes why she writes: "To discover myself, to preserve myself, to make myself, to achieve autonomy. To dispel the myths that I am a madwoman, a prophet, or poor suffering soul."[2] I, as an African American, use my language to do the same. I am not a poor suffering soul. I am an expressive person, and language is one of the ways I show it. Language and education are very important to both my grandfather and myself; but I believe that in his struggle for survival and resistance, he was forced into assimilation by the demands placed on him by white culture. This forced assimilation was so great it led him to believe that his own language was incorrect, and that the only proper way to live is the white way. Once he moved to the city from North Carolina, I think he forgot his own culture and replaced it with the white culture because at the time this was supposed to be the right way to survive.

Many years ago a college education was not available to African Americans, and this shows the difference between my form of traveling and my grandfather's. Two generations ago formal education was not available to him, so he feels that I should take everything I can get. Today formal education is allowed to me and I can easily attend a university. But what is the point of black students being able to attend the university if their needs are still not met? A few classes being given in African studies do not meet my needs. The same white administration that thinks they are doing us a favor by fulfilling their quotas and letting us come to their university, thinks they are doing us a favor by giving us a few classes. My grandfather fails to realize this and thinks I should be more appreciative of my education.

The decision that my grandfather made to come to New York City and conform to what white society expected of him forced me to make the decision that I will not conform to anyone's beliefs, cultures, or ideas—because I have my own. I do believe that had my grandfather stayed in the South and experienced the civil rights movement he would feel differently. "It's too easy, blaming it all on the white man or white feminists or society or our parents. What we say and what we do ultimately comes back to us. Let us own our responsibility, place it in our own hands and carry it with dignity and strength. No one is going to do my drudgery. I pick up, look after myself."[3] My language, culture, and identity belong to me. No one can force me to give up my identity or choose between that and white language and culture. If an entire people can endure the suffering and pain they faced during slavery, then I can fight to retain who I am.

Notes

1. bell hooks, *Black Looks: Race and Representation* (Boston: South End Press, 1992), 174.
2. Gloria Anzaldúa, "Speaking in Tongues: A Letter to Third World Women Writers," in *Words in Our Pockets: The Feminist Writers Guild Handbook on How to Gain Power, Get Published, and Get Paid,* ed. Celeste West (Paradise, Calif.: Dustbooks, 1985), 222.
3. Ibid., 225.

PART II

Our Parents, Ourselves

The essays in this section focus on parental immigration or migration experiences and speak to the impact of those experiences on the student authors themselves. More so than the authors in the last section, these students have been directly affected by the immigration process. The dominant theme that emerges is that of feeling torn between two cultures—the culture of one's parents and the broader American culture within which these students have grown up. Discrimination and a feeling of marginality have also influenced these students. Racial and cultural differences have set them apart from the dominant white culture in the United States far more than was the case for earlier immigrants whose experiences were recounted in Part I.

Each of the accounts is unique, but those by Melissa Algranati and Shana Rivas capture many of the themes that emerge in this section. The New York–born daughter of an Egyptian Jewish father and a Puerto Rican mother, Melissa has not grown up identifying with a single ethnic tradition. Being both Jewish and Hispanic challenges various stereotypes others hold and sets her somewhat apart from either group. Shana Rivas, as the daughter of a Puerto Rican father and an African American mother, deals with similar issues. Moving back and forth between New York City and Puerto Rico, Shana has had to learn English and Spanish and negotiate the cultural differences between city and country life.

Ultimately, she views her bicultural experience as a blessing, but there is no doubt it has also been a struggle.

Not only have these authors felt themselves caught between two worlds, their parents, too, have undergone an Americanization process. Peter Bosco, son of Italian immigrants, and Soo Y. Kim, a Korean immigrant, both comment on the way their parents tended to apply old-world standards in the treatment of older children but more Americanized standards with younger ones. For Shana Rivas and Sang-Hoon Kim there are significant differences between their parents in terms of their acceptance of American culture. Whether there are internal conflicts within the family or conflicts between family traditions and American expectations, these writers and their parents have been negotiating a difficult path between two worlds.

The attitudes of other Americans did not make that path any easier. These students felt the pain of discrimination more keenly than did classmates who were less conspicuous because they were white and more distant from their family's initial immigration. Cecilia Pineda, both of whose parents are Filipino, was the only Asian American in school when her family moved to the Washington, D.C., area, and she became the target of numerous racial slurs. Sang-Hoon Kim, New York–born son of Korean immigrants, fought one classmate who made repeated racial threats. During the fight, the classmate's friends lashed out at him with a variety of anti-Asian slurs. For these more recent immigrants, racial differences have been a source of pain and difficulty, but they have differing attitudes toward the dominant culture. Cecilia Pineda, Peter Bosco, and Ann Fenech express a strong sense of identification with American culture. Lynn Sugamura, despite the internment of her Japanese American parents during World War II, betrays no sense of resentment or bitterness. For Lizette Aguilar "the word assimilation has a negative meaning," and she identifies with her parents' rejection of much of dominant white Anglo culture in the United States. Between these extremes are those students who acknowledge the influence of two or even three cultures. Cultural assimilation and cultural pluralism coexist in these accounts as they do in American society at large.

Lynn Sugamura (UC San Diego 1983)

A Challenge of Loyalty

As a result of Japan's attack on Pearl Harbor on December 7, 1941, all persons of Japanese ancestry were directed by Executive Order 9066 to leave the California coastal area, an order that was enforced by Lt. Gen. John L. DeWitt of the Western Defense Command. Members of this group were forced to evacuate their homes by a certain date and were allowed only a minimal amount of baggage per person. Many families had no choice but to sell their belongings for as much money as they could get (usually very little), or entrust them to their non-Japanese friends. After gathering their possessions, they were boarded onto buses and trains and taken to various "relocation centers" located in California, Utah, Wyoming, Arkansas, and later, Colorado.

Both of my parents were born and raised in California. My father, whose parents hailed from Hawaii and Japan, was born Masaichi Tom (Sugamura) on October 8, 1928 in San Pedro, California. My mother, Teruyo (Kawaguchi), whose parents were both from Japan, was born on Terminal Island, California on April 15, 1929. She was raised in Los Angeles, but moved back to Terminal Island at age six. My mother and father were twelve and thirteen, respectively, when Pearl Harbor was bombed. The preeminent feeling among the majority of the people in every Japanese community (in regards to the bombing) was that of shock and disbelief. My mother remembers hearing the announcement on the radio as her family was getting ready to go to church.

At that time, the Kawaguchis were living on Terminal Island, which was

The Kawaguchi family, early 1934.

basically a Japanese fishing village. When my mother's family first heard of the evacuation procedures, they made plans to move in with relatives in Utah. They packed up a good deal of their clothing and belongings and sent them ahead. Unfortunately, a curfew was placed on the Japanese that required them to be indoors by a designated time. Another restriction was placed on the Japanese: they couldn't travel beyond a five-mile radius from their homes once the curfew was in effect, thus preventing the Kawaguchis from leaving the Southland. The curfew and travel restriction were primarily means of controlling emigration from the West Coast.

My "ji-chan" (grandfather Kawaguchi) was a fisherman and was, in a sense, kidnapped by FBI agents who raided many, if not all, of the Japanese fishing boats soon after the bombing of Pearl Harbor. The FBI took all alien fishermen to concentration (POW) camps where many were treated as criminals, along with the German soldiers who were being held there. Ji-chan was taken to a camp in North Dakota. The fishermen allegedly posed a threat to the United States; the government feared that these Japanese fishermen might have "signaled the enemy" while at sea.

During the time that many of the fishermen were in concentration camps, their families struggled. More so than the children, the Issei (first-generation) women suffered a great deal. Their grief for their missing husbands and the job of supporting the family was a rough experience. To make matters worse, most spoke no, or very little, English.

In May 1942 the Kawaguchis left their home to board a bus that was to take them to the Santa Anita (Racetrack) Relocation Center. This was only a temporary location until the camps were completed. It was at this time that my ji-chan was reunited with his family. They were, in fact, lucky to be reunited. Out of all those who were placed in the POW camps, those who were affiliated with any Japanese society, church, social, or community group along with the owners (Japanese) of any commercial fishing boats, were not released. Instead, they were relocated to another camp in Crystal City, Texas.

My father recalls being "herded like cattle" onto the buses by nervous GIs who were armed with guns and rifles. These same guards rode on the buses that took them to the Pomona (Fairgrounds) Assembly Center. When they arrived, they found out that they were to live in the horse stables.

Similarly, the Kawaguchis were bused to the Santa Anita (Racetrack) Assembly Center. When they arrived, all families had to wait in line to receive a "family number," which corresponded to their living quarters. My mother's family was more fortunate than my father's. Because they arrived relatively later than the other families, they lived in makeshift wood and tar paper barracks. If they had arrived earlier, they too would have had to live in the horse stables. Each family was also given a colored tag that corresponded to a specific mess hall where the family members were assigned to eat their meals.

At Santa Anita, my mother remembers how the older evacuees worked while the younger children attended school sessions in an outside classroom in the racetrack's grandstand. She recalls the dedication these people showed as they made camouflage nets for the U.S. Army. Although they were "incarcerated," they were still loyal and worked diligently for their country.

Both the Pomona and Santa Anita Assembly Centers closed down toward the end of the summer of 1942. The Sugamuras relocated to Jerome, Arkansas, but the camp closed down soon after their arrival. My father had an uncle in Amache, Colorado, so the family moved to the camp there. At this time, the Kawaguchis relocated to Heart Mountain, Wyoming.

Both of my parents remember their train rides as long. Because my parents were young, they don't recall much about knowing where they were going. While on the train, they do remember that they had to draw the blinds when they neared any city or town so the townspeople could not see who was aboard the train. While traveling in open country, however, they were able to open the blinds. My mother, looking back, thinks that the conductors probably took the longer "back routes" rather than the more direct routes to avoid arousing anyone's curiosity as to who was aboard the trains or why.

Heart Mountain, where the Kawaguchis were to live, was located in the desolate prairies of Wyoming. Sagebrush, rattlesnakes, and lonely barracks were all that was visible for miles around. The weather was terrible—"bitter" my mother called it—snow and blizzards for the majority of the winter.

Education was not neglected in the camps. Teachers were brought in from outside the gates and barbed wire to teach the "incarcerated" children. Classes were held in the barracks and were very crowded. After a year or so, a school building was built, along with a gymnasium at Heart Mountain. My mother recalls some sort of intramural athletic program being developed that later involved the non-Japanese people of Wyoming who went into the camps to participate.

As the months passed, many "community-type" activities and organizations arose. Churches were built and "police" forces organized. Eventually, weekly movies were shown, dances coordinated, and a canteen was built. Through the canteen many of the people ordered clothes and other "goodies" by way of mail-order catalogs from Montgomery Ward and Sears Roebuck.

Heart Mountain, Wyoming, where the Kawaguchi family was interned during World War II.

Many of the interned worked during the period they lived in the camps. The average rate of pay for regular laborers was about twelve dollars a month, sixteen dollars for white-collar workers, and nineteen dollars for doctors. An additional clothing allowance of two to four dollars per person was given each month. At Heart Mountain, my ba-chan (grandmother Kawaguchi) worked as a dishwasher, my ji-chan helped out in the kitchen, and Shizuyo (Sue), my mother's oldest sister, worked as a waitress.

During their incarceration many of the Japanese were very cooperative. They were generally a dedicated and hard-working group of people. They always felt that they were Americans despite the color of their skin. They never felt like the enemy. While in camp, many of those who were of age registered for the army and fought against Japan. One of the most noted groups was the 442d battalion, which was comprised solely of Japanese-Americans.

Toward the end of the internment period, there was quite a labor shortage in the states. A certain number of the interned were allowed to leave the camps and move out, provided they did not relocate to the West Coast. My Aunt Sue left Heart Mountain and moved to Chicago. Like many others who left camp to work, she was employed as a housegirl and went to school part-time. She attended Northwestern University for a short period. Similar to the majority of the Japanese young adults, my aunt's plans to attend college on a full-time basis had been ruined by the outbreak of the war and the forced internment.

The relocation camps officially closed during the summer of 1945. Many families left before they closed. However, those who had no relatives to move in with or had little money and could not afford to move, stayed until the last day. The Sugamuras left Amache, Colorado, and went back to San Pedro, California. My father's two older sisters, Chiyeko (Mary) and Fumi, moved to New York for a while. My father, being the youngest, stayed with his parents. My grandfather, who worked at a vegetable stand before the war, worked as a gardener after the camp. My grandmother worked in a fish cannery. My father attended San Pedro High School and graduated in 1946.

Unlike the Sugamuras, who moved back to their hometown, after the Kawaguchis left Heart Mountain in April of 1945 they lived and worked on a relative's farm in Utah. Ji-chan worked in a cannery away from the farm while ba-chan, my uncle (Tosh), and my mother worked on the farm. My mother's youngest sister, Miyeko (Mary), kept house and cooked and cleaned for the family. They worked in Utah all summer, but left for Albany, California, to avoid the terrible winter weather. The money they saved during their stay in Utah helped to set them up in California.

Block 21 kitchen staff, Heart Mountain, May 1944. Ba-chan Kawaguchi is first on left.

In Northern California, my mother attended Albany High School for the tenth grade. The following year, the Kawaguchis moved to the Virgil district of Hollywood, California. It was convenient for my mother's family because they always moved to areas where friends could help them settle in. Although neither ji-chan nor ba-chan spoke much English, they obtained jobs rather easily. Ji-chan worked as a gardener, and ba-chan did domestic work. My mother attended Belmont High School and graduated in 1947.

After settling in Southern California, my ji-chan asked if the family wanted to return to Japan. My mother remembers that Sue protested, "I'm an American citizen. Japan is not my country. The only country I know is America." Not wanting to leave his family behind, my ji-chan decided to stay in the United States. Once the legislation that restricted the Japanese from becoming citizens was lifted in 1952, my grandparents (from both sides of the family) attended citizenship school, passed the required examination, and became naturalized U.S. citizens.

Following high school graduation, my father attended Compton College. He was then drafted into the army for the Korean War and was stationed in Korea and Japan. After the war, he attended an aeronautical school and became an engineer. My mother, after graduating from Belmont High, attended Los Angeles Trade Technical College where she learned to sew. She worked for a while but soon decided that the sewing trade was for "old women." She decided to attended Metropolitan Business School and took up bookkeeping. She went out to work until she married. My parents met through a mutual friend some two years before my father was drafted into the army. They married on June 14, 1953.

In 1954 my oldest brother, Mark Masaji, was born. A year later, another son, David Michael, joined the family. In 1960, my parents were blessed with their first daughter, Lori Tomi. And in 1964, I, Lynn Julie, the youngest, was born. Though it was unfortunate for my grandfather to have only one son to carry on the Sugamura name, my father was fortunate to have two sons to maintain the family. Among all the nieces and nephews, my brother Mark was the first to get married. His wedding was in August of 1982.

All four children in the Sugamura family are high school graduates. My brother Mark graduated in 1972 and furthered his education at CSU Long Beach where he received a B.S. in zoology in 1976. My other brother, David, graduated in 1973, then attended Los Angeles Trade Technical College where he took up auto mechanics. My sister, Lori, graduated in 1978 and just recently graduated from CSU Los Angeles. She is now

Lynn Sugamura with her sister, cousins, and grandparents, Los Angeles, July 1969.

studying for her teaching credentials. I graduated in 1982, and am now attending UC San Diego with a major in biology.

Our entire family has discussed my parents' internment, and we look back on the situation as surprising and in a sense unfair, yet at the same time, possibly a "blessing in disguise." By this I mean that while unfair to the Japanese in that it stripped them of their inalienable rights as human beings as well as their right as citizens (for those who were U.S. citizens), it protected the Japanese from both verbal and physical abuse by individuals who might have taken it upon themselves to "defend" their country from the "Japs."

Many may expect the Japanese to be very bitter toward the Americans after this event, but I feel that most accept the fact that "what happened, happened" and that the government did what it had to do at the time. It may have been done primarily out of an act of fear more so than an act of defense, but one cannot alter history. It is only too bad that the U.S. government had to wait so long, more than thirty years, for hearings to take place regarding redress and reparation to repay the Japanese for what they had lost at the time of evacuation.

Shana R. Rivas (SUNY Binghamton 1990)

A Bicultural Experience

Puertorriqueña o moyeta? (Puerto Rican or black?) This is a question I have been confronted with for the past eleven years. My experience might be different from others because I am a product of two cultures. I sometimes wonder whether I should consider this a gift or the development of an identity problem. In this essay I focus on the migration experience of my father from Puerto Rico to Nueva York and that of my mother from Virginia to New York. I also add my migration experience and show how it has permitted me to identify my two cultures.

Papi was born just before the outbreak of World War II in Orocovis, Puerto Rico. Puerto Rico in the late 1930s, after thirty-five years of American administration, was a scene of almost unrelieved misery. The urban area of Puerto Rico (San Juan) did not suffer as much as the rural areas.

Orocovis was a rural town set in the high mountains in the southeast part of the island. The town had a population of about two thousand. The town of Orocovis was underdeveloped; housing and agriculture could have been better. The homes of many families were made of cement blocks with tin roofs and usually accommodated a family of five. There were no plumbing systems, and few homes had electricity. Most people in Orocovis made their living through agriculture, teaching, sewing, and selling homemade or homegrown products.

Papi came from a family of nine, including his parents, four daughters, and three sons. He was second oldest and was considered an important asset to the family. The first-born male in Puerto Rican tradition always had to help support the family, especially if they were not well off financially. Therefore, Papi was not able to attend school as a child.

Papi's childhood experience was more or less "bringing home the bread." He traveled with his father on occasions to different towns selling fruits, vegetables, poultry, and pork to store owners, and other times he spent around the home working in the backyard plot. At the age of fourteen, Papi took on full responsibility of the household after my grandfather died. Papi struggled as an uneducated, semi-skilled young adult to support his family. He worked from six in the morning until late in the evening selling his produce and working the land.

After several years of struggling to support *la familia,* Papi decided to enroll in school, but his plans to attend were interrupted. Papi's sister and other family members convinced him to go to New York City. He was not the first of the family to go, as my *tia* (aunt) Sophie had migrated to New York with her fiancé in search of a better life.

In 1958, at the age of twenty, Papi had convinced himself that he wanted to go to New York City. Leaving my grandmother and siblings with just enough money to survive for three months, Papi began what one would call "the Puerto Rican journey." He left with enough money to purchase a ticket and pay for his stay at my tia Sophie's home.

Papi arrived in New York City and made his way to Far Rockaway in Brooklyn. He knew no English except basic phrases such as "I no speeka English." He began searching for employment but that was very difficult for him as well as many other Puerto Rican males who came to New York City at that time. He was unskilled in many areas. Though he did not know many of the skills most employers were demanding during that period of time, Papi knew a great deal about agriculture and other outdoor jobs.

Time was drawing near to the end of the three months of support money Papi had left with his family back at home. He had to find a job to support himself and his family back on the island. In the summer of 1958 he landed a job as a gardener in Queens and Long Island. During the time he was laid off, Papi was a dishwasher in a diner.

As the year went by, Papi realized New York City was not what he had pictured it to be. He mentioned many times that Puerto Ricans, especially those with darker skin, were treated differently and discriminated against. For Papi, lack of education, lack of skills, and having dark skin worked against him in employment. The color of one's skin as a Puerto Rican played a major role in the caste and class system of this society.

A major factor that contributed to Papi's decision to return to the island was his inability to assimilate. He was restricted in doing many things because of his language and the color barrier. He wanted to be like an American man, but with no English it was impossible. Papi always said, "People in New York are not friendly and always made fun of Puerto Ricans." He had sensed Americans' attitudes toward Puerto Ricans of color and decided to return home one day.

After working three years at the diner and as a gardener he saved up enough money to send for his brother Andre and also to begin a small gardening business. His brother Andre was Papi's English tongue in the business. Hindy, a close friend and business partner, handled all the paperwork and dealt with the customers. Business went so well that Papi prolonged his stay until he found *Un Amor Americana*.

While gardening in Long Island, Papi met Mom, an all-American southern gal. Papi said, "I was able to communicate enough to sweep her off her feet." In October 1963, two months after they met, they married.

One of Papi's greatest aspirations was to become a *bodega* (store) owner. He fulfilled his aspiration, when he returned back home with a family and plans for the establishment of a bodega.

The migrant experience of a dark Puerto Rican on the mainland can be related to the experience of an African American migrant from the South. My mom migrated to New York from Virginia. She migrated during the last stages of the Great Migration from the South and at the peak of the civil rights movement—a period in which African Americans sought economic stability.

Mom was born in Branchville, Virginia, during the 1930s. She was the eldest of eleven children. Her father was a sharecropper and her mother was a housekeeper. Mom was reared during the latter part of the depression, when the United States was facing economic instability. This period affected many sharecroppers, because land rents were tremendous. Also in the 1940s there was a major flood that disrupted agriculture, and many families in lowland areas were displaced.

In the South, education was limited for many blacks on account of segregation and the need for extra hands in the fields. Mom was able to attend school and work the fields until junior high school. Mom had to quit school and take on a second job as a housekeeper as well as work in the fields. Her income was needed to help support the family. What her parents brought home was not enough to cover all expenses.

At eighteen Mom was able to find employment as a hairdresser, which released her from working in the fields daily. She worked as a hairdresser until the age of twenty. At this time Mom received an invitation from an aunt to come visit New York City. Mom mentioned that she was very hesitant to go because she was very much needed at home. In September 1957 Mom left for New York City with a ticket, one hundred dollars, and a dream. Her dream was to complete school and become economically stable. Her first stop in New York City was in New Hyde Park, Long Island, where she resided and also held a job as a housekeeper for a wealthy Jewish lawyer.

After several months in New York City, Mom discovered that urban life was going to be a difficult adjustment. She really did not like the urban lifestyle. Mom said, "It was a fast pace of life, too many people and too many large buildings." Mom had the southern lifestyle instilled in her, and coming from what one would call the "deep woods" of the South, it was very difficult for her to adapt to her new urban life.

There was a period in which Mom faced discrimination while in New York City. Mom lived in an area where blacks were not welcome to live unless employed as domestic help. Although she had a place to stay, Mom wanted a home of her own. While she was looking in areas of New Hyde Park, many doors were closed, telling her "this neighborhood does not rent to Negroes." Confronting incidents such as these led Mom to believe that New York City was no place for her.

While I was discussing Mom's migration experience with her a question came to mind. I asked Mom why would she have preferred to go back South, when black hatred was more prominent in the South. She replied, "Where I am from although you're black, southern whites did not treat you like northerners. And I also prefer to be with my family even if I have to struggle. I could not stand being alone and afraid."

Although Mom regretted coming to New York City, she managed to overcome those incidents and better her condition. Mom enrolled in school and was able to obtain a high school diploma. She continued her education and became a certified food examiner. Two years after receiving her certification Mom met Papi and they were married. They then settled in Queens where three of the four children were born.

My parents were able to make ends meet, but were not comfortable with their social status in the United States. At this point, in 1965, Papi and Mom moved to Puerto Rico and established a better social class status. Mom managed to communicate with what knowledge of Spanish she learned through school, my Uncle Andre, and Papi. She did not like Puerto Rico and had a difficult time assimilating. Mom could not find work and it was very hard for her to get around without my father.

In 1969 I came along, reared in the traditions of the "old generation." I was the only child born and reared in Puerto Rico, and I spent most of my time with my step-grandfather. I spoke only Spanish and grew up in that culture. Puerto Rico was my first home for ten years. Papi always made me aware of my second home, which I knew as "America–Nueva York." I knew it was a far-off place and much different from Puerto Rico. In August 1978 I was part of the "second generation of the Puerto Rican journey." I boarded a plane for New York City, scared and wondering what would be awaiting me on the other side of the Caribbean. I feared that people would not like me and that I would not be able to adapt to the American culture.

In New York City, I struggled very hard trying to "fit in." Although I did not know the English language, I would try to make friends anyway. I had a difficult time through school for the first two years. Learning English was quite a frustrating experience. I felt like I was in a silent world. I would cry and laugh out of embarrassment. It was a battle that I eventually won.

Once I was fully established with the language, I faced an identity crisis. Many times people questioned me, "Are you fully black?" Or "Where are you from? You have an accent." I realized I was a product of two different cultures and it was noticed. I began weighing both, knowing that only one would be dominant. At one point in my life I wanted to be known as a black girl born in New York City. It was possible; I had all the features, but there was the "accent." This accent identified me as a person of both black and Puerto Rican roots.

It was not until I visited Virginia and spent time with my maternal grandparents that I accepted who I was and where I descended from. My grandparents told me tales of many of my ancestors, who lived long after slavery until my mom was a child—tales from which black history has developed. I was also able to see the factual basis of the tales, which led me to believe that I was gifted with a bicultural experience.

I have accepted both cultures, but to Americans I would either be black or Puerto Rican—most of the time black. My parents always extended themselves in teaching me my roots and helping me to accept them. But assimilating into one was very difficult without forgetting the other.

My father did not try hard enough to assimilate. He returned to Puerto Rico with no intention of returning. My mom accepted the urban lifestyle although she still regrets coming to New York.

Despite all the moving around my parents did in adjusting to New York and Puerto Rican culture, they overcame it all. My mom is doing well as a chocolate inspector and Papi as a self-employed businessman in Puerto Rico. I still have gripes about my father not learning English and assimilating to American culture just as I have done. I struggled and fought to assimilate, identify myself, and be able to feel blessed with a "bicultural experience."

Cecilia Pineda (UC San Diego 1978)

My Family History

Tracing my historical beginning was not as easy as I thought it would be. It proved to be a fascinating experience just to hear the names of my ancestors, yet a frustrating search for those I will probably never know. Through remembrances of my parents I was able to learn about my maternal great-great-grandparents, my paternal grandparents, and of our immigration to the United States.

My family is of Philippine descent and most of my ancestors are full-blooded Filipinos. On my mother's side, my grandparents were Patrocino Feliciano and Lourdes David. They lived in San Fernando, Pampanga, which is one of the many provinces on the island of Luzon, Philippines. He worked as a foreman for a construction company, but during the Japanese occupation in World War II, he was forced to quit the company and take on odd jobs such as buying and selling goods. My grandmother ran a grocery store. She has been living in Manila, the capital of the Philippines, since my grandfather died of a heart attack in 1967.

The parents of my grandfather were Flaviano Feliciano and Ramona Tiomico. The name Tiomico is Chinese, therefore she was of Chinese descent. My great-grandfather worked as an overseer with a lumber company. They, too, lived in San Fernando.

Leoncio David and Gertrudes Quiazon were the parents of my grandmother. They also lived in San Fernando. Leoncio worked in the civil service of the Philippines as a clerk. Gertrudes worked as a seamstress in a dress shop. She was a "mestiza," half-Filipino and half-Spanish. Most names of Filipinos are Spanish in origin because the Philippine Islands were a Spanish territory from 1565 to 1898, and intermarriage produced the many Spanish surnames.

The parents of Gertrudes, my great-great-grandparents, were Angelo Quiazon and Marcela Canlas. Angelo was of Spanish descent and also worked as a clerk for the civil service. Marcela sold vegetables and fruits at a local market. The area they lived in—San Fernando, where most of my maternal descendants are from—had a rural, agrarian way of life. One form of transportation consisted of horse-drawn carriages called *calesas.* For ten centavos, roughly one and a half pennies, one could ride anywhere in a "Jeepney," a brightly painted jeep, or a tricycle that holds two passengers. Even today these modes of transportation are in existence because most people in the provinces are too poor to own cars. The houses were built of wood. You rarely saw lawns since each family usually owned some chickens and other farm animals. Families sold their produce and bought their usual supplies at big open-air markets, which still operate at the local level of most provinces. The way of life was essentially very simple. People made do with what they had. Technology has modernized such things as communication (although Filipino families rarely have telephones), transportation, and types of occupations, and has generally raised the standard of living in the Philippines, but it has not affected the provinces.

There are areas where the word "technology" has never been heard of. I am speaking of the barrios, where my father's ancestors originated. My grandfather Silvestre Pineda was employed as a barber. My grandmother was Nieves Higonia, and she took in laundry to help support the family. Their existence can be described as "barely enough to get by." The housing consisted of pieces of plywood slapped together. It barely provided shelter from the seasonal rains and humid summers. Their diet consisted of fish, rice, and vegetables bought daily from the market since they had no refrigerator. Everyone in the family worked as soon as they were old enough, to finance the family's needs.

My father used to work in the rice fields every afternoon and take care of the caribous. Throughout my childhood he has always reminded me of the good things God has provided, and that I should be grateful because, as a child, he never enjoyed any of the "basic" luxuries we have today such as television, stereos, a closet of clothes, and so on. My grandparents died of heart attacks while my father was in elementary school, so he was never told of his ancestors. His grandparents also died early, even before he knew their "legal" names, those outside of Grandma and Grandpa. My father,

Luis Higonia Pineda, was then put under the care of my great-uncle, Abelardo De Ocera, and his wife, Presentacion. He finished high school and worked his way through two years of college at Far Eastern University in Manila. There he met Lourdes David Feliciano, my mother. My father eventually quit college to enlist in the U.S. Navy, thus embarking on a life of constant mobility. My parents were the first of my family to immigrate to the United States.

I can clearly remember all the different places I've lived, and the ethnicity of each location. I think of it in terms of my years in school because I've never been in the same school for more than one year, except for my junior and senior years in high school. I was born in Subic Bay Naval Base, the Philippines, while my father was stationed there. A year later, in 1959, he was transferred to Bremerton, Washington, where my sister was born. This was the first time my mother had ever been to the United States, and she remembers her emotions vividly.

To some extent my father had been exposed to the American way of life through his work at the base, but he remembers feeling alienated, of being in a strange land. He "felt powerless among the tall buildings, rushing traffic, and busy atmosphere." But gradually through everyday life within this culture, his alienation transformed into a feeling of "belonging." For my mother, this transformation was a similar experience. She remembers "being in awe of America's vastness." She was impressed by the orderliness of everything and how technology provided so many conveniences. For instance, she had never used a washing machine or a refrigerator before, or even a vacuum cleaner. She had no feeling of alienation, just a need to readjust herself to this new environment. We stayed in Washington for two years until we were then transferred to Yokuska, Japan. My two brothers were born there, and all I remember about Japan is the Buddha, and how cold it was during the winter.

After two years in Japan, we transferred to Alameda, California. I was in the second grade and it was around then that I clearly felt like everyone else, like every other American child. I had known no other way of life so I naturally assumed that this was how it was meant to be. After leaving Alameda, we lived for a year in Coronado and for a year in San Diego. Then in 1969 my father was stationed in the Philippines for three years. Of course we all went with him, and I got a chance to learn the history and culture of my native land, not to mention meeting all of my relatives for the first time! It was one of the most memorable experiences of my life because I had the best of both worlds. We lived on the base where my American culture continued, and every other weekend, we would journey to

Cecilia Pineda and her mother in Bremerton, Washington, September 1959.

Manila to visit my grandmother. After three years, I was able to understand some Tagalog, the native language, as well as Pampango, the dialect that my parents still speak at home. I love all the food and Philippine delicacies. We did a lot of sightseeing and visited the areas where my parents grew up.

Manila is a very cosmopolitan city, much like Los Angeles, so the adjustments were not difficult. What surprised me was how poor the area is where my father is from. The people barely survive—one-room shacks line the dirt streets. There is no running water, and rats and mosquitoes infest the area. My father is not proud of this place; rather, he is proud of migrating to America and of the life it has brought our family.

During my ninth and tenth grades, we moved to Washington D.C., a completely different environment. I saw snow for the first time there during the winter. The racial makeup was also a change. I and the whites who lived on base were bused to an all-black school in Seat Pleasant, Maryland. It is hard to believe, but I was the only Oriental in the whole school. This brought me a lot of attention, both good and bad. Since I was neither black nor white, being in the middle made it easier to make friends with both races. To blacks, I was not white and to whites, I was not black. However, I found that some people, both black and white, were prejudiced against Orientals as a whole. I got called everything from "Chink" to "Jap" but they never even bothered to ask about my nationality. I'm sure if they did they probably would have learned something. Nevertheless, I enjoyed Washington because of the history that seemed to emanate from the city, and the many friends I made.

Our traveling days ended in 1974 when my father retired from the Navy to settle in San Diego. We love California for all the reasons I'm sure everyone knows. More importantly, we love America for all the good things and the opportunities it has afforded us. My parents had a choice of where to spend their future, and in choosing the United States, assimilation was just a period of willing adjustment. I have always lived in and with this culture, and I cannot imagine living any other way.

Melissa Algranati (SUNY Binghamton 1994)

Being an Other

Throughout my whole life, people have mistaken me for other ethnic backgrounds, rather than for what I really am. I learned at a young age that there are not too many Puerto Rican, Egyptian Jews out there. For most of my life I have been living in two worlds, and at the same time I have been living in neither. When I was young I did not realize that I was unique, because my family brought me up with a healthy balance of Puerto Rican and Sephardic customs. It was not until I took the standardized PSAT exam that I was confronted with the question: "Who am I?" I remember the feeling of confusion as I struggled to find the right answer. I was faced with a bad multiple-choice question in which there was only supposed to be one right answer, but more than one answer seemed to be correct. I did not understand how a country built on the concept of diversity could forget about its most diverse group, inter-ethnic children. I felt lost in a world of classification. The only way for me to take pride in who I am was to proclaim myself as an other, yet that leaves out so much. As a product of a marriage only a country like America could create, I would now try to help people understand what it is like to be a member of the most underrepresented group in the country, the "others."

My father, Jacques Algranati, was born in Alexandria, Egypt. As a Sephardic Jew, my father was a minority in a predominantly Arab world. Although in the minority, socially my father was a member of the upper middle class and lived a very comfortable life. As a result of strong French influence in the Middle Eastern Jewish world, my father attended a French private

Melissa Algranati's father, Jacques, at right, with his older brother, Nissim, in Egypt in 1958.

school. Since Arabic was the language of the lower class, the Algranati family spoke French as their first language. My whole family is polyglot, speaking languages from the traditional Sephardic tongue of Ladino to Turkish and Greek. My grandfather spoke seven languages. Basically, my father grew up in a close-knit Sephardic community surrounded by family and friends.

However, in 1960 my father's world came to a halt when he was faced with persecution on an institutional level. As a result of the Egyptian-Israeli conflict, in 1956 an edict was issued forcing all foreign-born citizens and Jews out of Egypt. Although my father was a native-born citizen of the country, because of a very strong anti-Jewish sentiment, his citizenship meant nothing. So in 1960 when my family got their exit visas, as Jews had done since the time of the Inquisition, they packed up and left the country as one large family group.

Unable to take many possessions or much money with them, my father's family, like many Egyptian Jews, immigrated to France. They proceeded to France because they had family who were able to sponsor them. Also, once in France my family hoped to be able to receive a visa to America much sooner, since French immigration quotas to the United States were much higher than those in Egypt. Once in France my family relied on the generosity of a Jewish organization, the United Jewish Appeal. For nine months my father lived in a hotel sponsored by the United Jewish Appeal and attended French school until the family was granted a visa to the United States.

Since my father's oldest brother came to the United States first with his wife, they were able to sponsor the rest of the family's passage over. The Algranati family eventually settled in Forest Hills, Queens. Like most immigrants, my family settled in a neighborhood filled with immigrants of the same background. Once in the United States, my father rejoined many of his old friends from Egypt, since most Egyptian Jewish refugees followed a similar immigration path. At the age of fourteen my father and his group of friends were once again forced to adjust to life in a new country, but this time they had to learn a new language in order to survive. Like many of his friends, my father was forced to leave the comforts and luxuries of his world for the hardships of a new world. But as he eloquently puts it, once his family and friends were forced to leave, there was really nothing to stay for.

Like my father, my mother is also an immigrant; however my parents come from very different parts of the world. Born in Maniti, Puerto Rico, my mom spent the first five years of her life in a small town outside of San Juan. Since my grandfather had attended private school in the United States when he was younger, he was relatively proficient in English. Like many immigrants, my grandfather came to the United States first, in or-

Five-year-old Maria Louisa Pinto, Melissa Algranati's mother, with her thirteen-year-old sister, in a park in Puerto Rico.

der to help establish the family. After securing a job and an apartment, he sent for my grandmother, and three weeks later my mother and her fourteen-year-old sister came.

Puerto Ricans are different from many other people who come to this country, in the sense that legally they are not considered immigrants. Because Puerto Rico is a commonwealth of the United States, Puerto Ricans are granted automatic U.S. citizenship. So unlike most, from the day my mother and her family stepped on U.S. soil they were considered citizens. The only problem was that the difference in language and social status led "real" Americans not to consider them citizens.

As a result of this unique status, my mother faced many hardships in this new country. From the day my mother entered first grade, her process of Americanization had begun. Her identity was transformed. She went from being Maria Louisa Pinto to becoming Mary L. Pinto. Not only was my mother given a new name when she began school, but a new language was forced upon her as well. Confronted by an Irish teacher, Mrs. Walsh, who was determined to Americanize her, my mother began her uphill battle with the English language. Even until this day my mother recalls her traumatic experience when she learned how to pronounce the word "run":

"Repeat after me, run."

"Rrrrrrrrun."

"No, Mary, run."

"Rrrrrrrrun."

No matter how hard my mother tried she could not stop rolling her "r's." After several similar exchanges Mrs. Walsh, with a look of anger on her face, grabbed my mother's cheeks in her hand and squeezed as she repeated in a stern voice, "RUN!" Suffice it to say my mother learned how to speak English without a Spanish accent. It was because of these experiences that my mother made sure the only language spoken in the house or to me and my sister was English. My parents never wanted their children to experience the pain my mother went through just to learn how to say the word "run."

My mother was confronted with discrimination not only from American society but also from her community. While in the United States, my mother lived in a predominantly Spanish community. On first coming to this country her family lived in a tenement in the Bronx. At the age of twelve my mother was once more uprooted and moved to the projects on the Lower East Side. As one of the first families in a predominantly Jewish building, it was a step up for her family.

It was not her environment that posed the biggest conflict for her; it was her appearance. My mother is what people call a "white Hispanic." With her blond hair and blue eyes my mother was taken for everything but a Puerto Rican. Once my mother perfected her English, no one suspected her ethnicity unless she told them. Since she was raised to be above the ghetto, never picking up typical "Hispanic mannerisms," she was able to exist in American society with very little difficulty. Because of a very strong and protective mother and the positive influence and assistance received from the Henry Street Settlement, my mother was able to escape the ghetto. As a result of organizations like Henry Street, my mother was given opportunities such as fresh air camps and jobs in good areas of the city, where she was able to rise above the drugs, alcohol, and violence that consumed so many of her peers.

As a result of her appearance and her upbringing, my mother left her people and the ghetto to enter American society. It was here as an attractive "white" female that my mother and father's two very different worlds merged. My parents, both working on Wall Street at the time, were introduced by a mutual friend. Since both had developed a rather liberal view, the differences in their backgrounds did not seem to be a major factor. After a year of dating my parents decided to get engaged.

Although they were from two different worlds, their engagement seemed to bring them together. Growing up in the midst of the Jewish community of the Lower East Side, my mother was constantly influenced by the beauty of Judaism. Therefore, since my mother never had much connection with Catholicism and had never been baptized, she decided to convert to Judaism and raise her children as Jews. The beauty of the conversion was that no one in my father's family forced her to convert; they accepted her whether she converted or not. As for my mother's family, they too had no real objections to the wedding or conversion. To them the only thing that mattered was that my father was a nice guy who made my mom happy. The most amusing part of the union of these two different families came when they tried to communicate. My father's family is descended from Spanish Jewry where many of them spoke an old Castilian-style Spanish, while my mother's family spoke a very modern Caribbean-style Spanish. To watch them try to communicate in any language other than English was like watching a session of the United Nations.

It was this new world, that of Puerto Rican Jewry, my parents created for me and my sister, Danielle. Resembling both my parents, having my mother's coloring with my father's features, I have often been mistaken for various ethnicities. Possessing light hair and blue eyes, I am generally perceived as the "all-American" girl. Occasionally I have been mistaken for Ital-

Wedding picture, Jacques Algranati and Maria Louisa Pinto, 1970.

ian since my last name, Algranati, although Sephardic, has a very Italian flair to it. I have basically lived a chameleon-like existence for most of my life.

As a result of my "otherness," I have gained "acceptance" in many different crowds. From this acceptance I have learned the harsh reality behind my "otherness." I will never forget the time I learned about how the parents of one of my Asian friends perceived me. From very early on, I gained acceptance with the parents of one of my Korean friends. Not only did they respect me as a person and a student, but her father even went so far as to consider me like "one of his daughters." I will always remember how I felt when I heard they made one of their daughters cancel a party because she had invited Hispanics. Even when my friend pointed out that I, the one they loved, was Hispanic they refused to accept it. Even today to them I will always be Jewish and not Puerto Rican because to them it is unacceptable to "love" a Puerto Rican.

Regardless of community, Jewish or Puerto Rican, I am always confronted by bigots. Often I am forced to sit in silence while friends utter in ignorance stereotypical responses like: "It was probably some spic who stole it," or "You're just like a Jew, always cheap."

For the past three years I have worked on the Lower East Side of Manhattan at the Henry Street Settlement. Basically my mother wanted me to support the organization that helped her get out of the ghetto. Unlike when my mother was there, the population is mostly black and Hispanic. So one day during work I had one of my fellow workers say to me "that is such a collegian white thing to say." I responded by saying that his assumption was only partially correct and asked him if considered Puerto Rican to be white. Of course he doubted I was any part Hispanic until he met my cousin who "looks" Puerto Rican. At times like these I really feel for my mother, because I know how it feels not to be recognized by society for who you are.

Throughout my life I do not think I have really felt completely a part of any group. I have gone through phases of hanging out with different crowds trying in a sense to find myself. Basically, I have kept my life diverse by attending both Catholic-sponsored camps and Hebrew school at the same time. Similar to my parents, my main goal is to live within American society. I choose my battles carefully. By being diverse I have learned that in a society that is obsessed with classification the only way I will find my place is within myself. Unfortunately, society has not come to terms with a fast-growing population, the "others." Therefore when asked the infamous question: "Who are you?" I respond with a smile, "a Puerto Rican Egyptian Jew." Contrary to what society may think, I know that I am somebody.

Sang-Hoon Kim (SUNY Binghamton 1994)

Discovering My Ethnic Roots

I am a second-generation Korean American. Both of my parents immigrated to the United States from Seoul, South Korea, for similar reasons: the limited freedoms and the lack of economic opportunities in the decades after the Korean War caused them to seek better ways of life in America. When they arrived in the foreign land, they almost immediately faced racial prejudice and discrimination. Both my father and my mother, at some point in their lives, had to struggle to find out what it means to be Korean American. It surprised me how their struggle with their ethnic identities was so similar to my own as a native-born American.

In 1940 my father was born Kim Kee-Jung in Pyongyang, Korea, the second son of a land developer working for the Japanese. It was a period when Korea was under harsh Japanese colonial rule and my grandfather was forced to serve their government. The Korean language was banned; anything written or even spoken in Korean was strictly forbidden. From the beginning of my father's life, his own ethnicity was in jeopardy. However, my grandparents made sure that his first words were Korean. In 1944, after violent demonstrations against Japanese authority by the Korean people, the government required that all Koreans adopt Japanese names, thus obliterating Korea as a country. My father's family name was changed from Kim to Toshiki. After the defeat of Japan in 1945, the Korean language was reinstated and all names were changed back.

Shortly after the ethnicity crisis, Korea was divided into two parts; the northern part became Communist and the southern part became democratic under the influence of the United States. My grandfather's dream was to own his own land and property, and to raise his children in a free society, so he found no future under Kim Il-Sung's regime. The partitioning of Korea transformed the country into two different nations with two different ideologies. My father's family moved to the South, leaving some relatives and friends behind. Little did they know that after the Korean War they would never be allowed to communicate with them again. According to my father, the trip to Seoul was indeed his first immigration.

My father spent most of his youth in Seoul. The political turmoil in South Korea influenced his decision to study and live in America. The government strictly limited freedom of expression as well as monetary transactions. Even wages and salaries were controlled. As his father had seen no future in North Korea, my father saw no future in South Korea. His father encouraged his emigration and supported him financially for his first year in America.

In August 1963 my father arrived in America and became a graduate student in accounting at Columbia University in New York City. However, he dropped out after two years because of the untimely death of his father and the need to earn more money right away. He moved to Flushing, a district in Queens, and for the next ten years, he found various jobs to support himself. He was a waiter, a store manager, and finally a salesman for Ovaltine. His ultimate goal was to earn enough money to become an entrepreneur and start his own business.

My father moved to Flushing primarily because it was heavily populated by Koreans. This permitted him to work for Korean store owners and communicate effectively. Association with people of the same culture, the same language, and the same ethnicity made life much easier and more productive; he was able to go on living without the problems of misunderstanding.

In January 1974 his mother called and told him to come back to Seoul. She had found a possible wife for him. Her name was Park In-Sook. Even though arranged marriages were well on their way toward extinction, she was a traditionalist. However, no one was forced to marry anyone. My paternal grandmother was friends with Park In-Sook's aunt. They fell in love after all. For eight months, they kept in touch through letters and phone calls. In October 1974 they were wed in Seoul.

My mother agreed to live with my father in America since it was traditional that the wife move in with the husband. My mother's adaption to American society was very difficult. The most difficult obstacle, as with most other immigrants, was learning the English language. In contrast to my father, who took English classes for two years before immigrating, my

Sang-Hoon Kim's parents at their engagement party, Seoul, 1974.

mother literally stepped off the plane without knowing any English. She depended entirely on my father for communication and translation. The English grammar was so different from that of Korean that she thought it was impossible to completely learn the language and to keep her way of thinking. To this day she still has some difficulty with English grammar.

Both faced much racial harassment while living in this country. It was common to be stared at wherever they went. Some people were not hesitant to spew out racial slurs such as "go back to China" and "no chinks allowed" because Asian Americans had very little power in society and there were few consequences for racism against Asian Americans. On numerous occasions, they were "forgotten" by service personnel in stores and in restaurants. Despite frustrations, my mother said that they remained strong and accepted the fact that there will always be prejudices.

I was born in June 1975 in Flushing, New York. I am the first person from either family to be born and raised in America. When I was three, my family moved to Ossining, New York, in Westchester County, just above New York City. There my father had the opportunity to purchase his own store. We still live in Ossining to this day. Despite the low population of Asians in our new town, we still maintain our cultural traditions. I remember going to New York City every weekend to shop for Korean food and to attend Korean church. Until I started school, Korean was the only language I spoke at home. I preferred to use the Korean language and preferred Korean food. Integration into the town was difficult; for example, my parents kept on bowing rather than shaking hands with non-Koreans because of habit.

Even though I learned some English at home, by the time I started kindergarten, I knew very little when compared to other children. I have no clear memory of how I eventually started to use English as second nature. I know that it was not difficult, probably because of my age. Through the next several years, my English-speaking ability significantly improved and even surpassed that of my Korean. I only had friends of European descent. I began to prefer American foods such as hamburgers, steaks, and pizza over rice, kimchi, and soybean stew. My thinking and attitudes were "American"; I thought and solved problems in my head using English. I forgot the shape of my eyes and considered myself fully "American." Despite occasional racial verbal attacks I considered myself to be an average American and was very proud of it.

It wasn't until high school that I found out how cruel people can be to someone of a different race. My parents enrolled me in a predominantly white Catholic school where there was only one Asian American in each grade level. Most of my classmates were tolerant, and making friends was generally easy, but the memories of my freshman year are still ones of hatred and intense bitterness. One student constantly made racial threats, and when I could not endure them any more, we fought. His friends were present and I remember them yelling, "Get him back for Vietnam," "Pound him into chop suey," and "Remember Hiroshima." Those words hurt just as much as the punches I received. The dean finally came and stopped the fight. My opponent was expelled from school, and I was let off with a stern warning and a week's detention. Throughout the year the name-calling continued. For the first time in my life I felt completely rejected by almost everyone who wasn't part of my family. I was angry at the world.

I felt ashamed of my race. I actually asked myself, "Of all people, why am I Asian? Why me?" Instead of taking action I continued to feel sorry for myself. I started to feel alienated from my friends and even became distrustful of them. That fight was a rude awakening to the reality of being Asian American in the United States. I even began to hate all white people. I did not realize that it was wrong and hypocritical of me to accuse an entire race based on the actions of an ignorant few.

Because of my depression, I felt that I had to learn more of my Korean heritage, so I attempted to rediscover my own ethnicity. That first year of high school was one of severe identity crisis. Being a person of a different race in this country is hard enough, but to actually go back and embrace one's own culture is even more difficult. With the help of my mother, I rediscovered the Korean language by watching Korean programs and by learning the alphabet—it was not as difficult as I had thought. My mother stressed that this is who I really am. I still have Korean blood, but that does not mean that I cannot be the product of the best from each culture.

I am now a student at Binghamton University majoring in biology. I have both Korean and non-Korean friends; however I actually had to attempt to make Korean friends by joining a cultural club. My biggest fear was that I would not be accepted because I was too "white," or too "American." To my surprise, most Korean American students experienced the same things I did; they all remember experiencing racial hatred, rejecting their culture, and going through an identity crisis. For the first time, I met people who were similar to me. I finally found people who I could truly relate to as a second-generation Korean American.

My parents' struggle was to assimilate successfully into American society while still maintaining their cultural heritage; ironically, this was my struggle all along. Understandably, my parents consider themselves to be more Korean than American. I, however, think of myself as a true American. America is a nation with its history based on immigrants from widely differing origins; the story of the American immigrant *is* American history. I am truly fortunate that I am a product of two unique cultures. Sometime I hope to visit and tour Korea, the land of my roots. I shall always be proud to be an Asian American.

Peter Bosco (SUNY Binghamton 1990)

The Experiences of My Parents in Italy and America

In September 1945 my mother, Anna Marie Lauriero, was born in the town of Altamura in the province of Bari, Italy, the second of four children. She lived with her family on a subsistence farm that her father, Donato, had received as a dowry when marrying my grandmother Maria. This farm grew enough food to feed the family, but created little, if any, surplus. In addition to working on his own farm, my grandfather worked on the farms of others to bring in extra income.

Life in Italy was simple for my mother. She went to school until the fifth grade. While she would have liked to continue her education, my grandmother had other plans for her. My mother was put to work sewing piecework for a local factory. She was ten at the time.

Anna Marie knew of America. Her mother's sister, Rose, had come to America with her husband and family in 1930. At Christmas and birthdays, she would send my mother and her siblings five dollars each. This gesture alone was enough to make the Laurieros imagine a land of plenty. Rose invited my mother's family to live in America when my mother was seven (1953). The entire family was thrilled at the prospect of moving to America. However, immigrating proved impossible at the time, for the United States was severely restricting immigration during this period. My mother blames the Eisenhower administration for her not being able to come to this country.

My mother's family kept applying for visas. In 1963 my mother, her two younger brothers (Paul and Mike), and their parents went to the

Anna Lauriero with her mother, Maria, in Bari, Italy, 1961.

American consul in Naples. There they were given thorough physicals, given clean bills of health, and granted visas (her eldest brother, Freddy, had married and moved to Switzerland). They came to America by steamship in 1963. The trip took twelve days. Mike and Anna Marie were seasick during part of the voyage, but Paul was sick the entire time. Otherwise, the ship itself was relatively comfortable. Everyone had a bed and plenty to eat.

Upon arriving in America, the family moved into Rose's house in Bensonhurst, a predominantly Italian neighborhood in Brooklyn, New York. They rented the attic (three rooms) for two and a half years before they could move to their own apartment.

My mother quickly settled into her new environment. Anxious to communicate better in this new country, she went to night school for three years to learn English. Within two weeks of coming to America she found work as a seamstress at a factory, first in Manhattan (for one year), then in Brooklyn. Most of the other workers in the factory were also Italian immigrant women. Interestingly enough, this is where discrimination was worst. The women often formed little groups that gossiped and mocked other workers. These women often picked on my mother. Most of the other women had immigrated many years earlier or were born in America. However, most of them spoke only Italian and clung tenaciously to the ways of the Old World, according to my mother. They mocked her when she spoke English. The reason they treated my mother and others like her this way was because she was young, a new immigrant who was attempting to become more American. They felt she wasn't proud of her heritage because she was learning to speak English. They also saw new workers as a threat to their jobs.

My mother also had a hard time at home. She gave her mother twenty-five dollars a week to pay rent and bills. She often wanted to go out with friends to the movies or the amusement park at nearby Coney Island, and thus came into conflict with her parents, who felt she should only work and do as she was told until she had a husband to obey. In 1966 she met her future husband and my father, Anthony Bosco.

Anthony Bosco was born in 1937 in Castellammare del golfo, a fishing town on the west coast of the island of Sicily. His father, Peter, was a blacksmith and his mother, Josephine, owned and ran a grocery store. Most of the other people in this town were subsistence farmers or fishermen. My father was the second of four children. He was educated until the seventh grade. He started helping his father at the age of five in his blacksmith shop, and became a full apprentice when he left school. He worked at the

Anthony Bosco, age fourteen, in Sicily.

Bosco family members in Sicily in the early 1960s. Left to right: Peter Bosco's uncle Salvatore, his grandparents, his father.

shop until the age of twenty-one, when he was drafted into the army. My father wanted to go into the army so he could leave his town and see the world. During his eighteen months in the army, both of his sisters married. His older sister, Antoinette, married a local businessman. Frances, his younger sister, married an Italian American from Bensonhurst, who had come back to Sicily specifically to find a wife.

When Anthony left the army, he returned briefly to his home. He soon left again with some friends to seek work in Turin. He found a job in construction, which he gave up after two months. He returned to his home and applied for a job with the Fiat factory in Palermo, Sicily's biggest city. He was hired. In 1963, while he was working for Fiat, his parents and his younger brother, Sal, immigrated to America, where they lived with Frances. My father, at the urging of his parents, came to America in 1966 by airplane. He too lived with his sister for three months, until he, his parents, and Sal moved into an apartment above Tony's fish store, where his parents worked. When my father came to America, Tony found him work in an auto repair shop fixing cars, despite his lack of experience. While his employers said they would train and supervise him, he was often left to guess at what he should do to fix a car. He eventually lost his job because he didn't do his job well.

He too felt discrimination, mostly from other Italians who had been in this country for a while. This discrimination manifested itself in his difficulty in finding a job. Others who had been in his position when they came to this country were unsympathetic and looked upon him as different.

With the aid of a *paesan* (a friend originally from his hometown in Sicily), Anthony eventually found another job, this time assembling kitchen appliances. This job did not satisfy him. He scanned *Il Progresso* (an Italian newspaper published in Brooklyn) continuously, hoping to find a better job. He saw an ad for an auto mechanic at the garage where he had worked. He asked for a second chance and explained to them how he wanted to learn to fix cars. He was given a second chance and eventually proved to be the best mechanic they had.

While my father was training as a mechanic, he began to miss Sicily. He was having difficulty assimilating into this new country and felt that he was different. He clung to his culture. He wanted to go back to Italy. My grandmother did not want her son leaving her and going back. She knew that the one thing that could keep him in America was a wife. My parents were introduced to each other by a mutual friend of my mother and paternal grandmother at a dinner party in March 1966. With a bit of encouragement from my father's mother and my mother's friend, the two met and grew fond of each other. Their courtship followed Italian tradition. The two were never alone. My mother's mother and her younger brother Mike accompanied them wherever they went. They did not have a moment of privacy until they married in September 1967.

Both of my parents went into the relationship with the intention of marrying. My mother, who was only twenty-two at the time, would already have been considered an old maid back in Altamura. Though she was attempting to become more American in many ways, she felt the pressure to marry carried over from the Old World. In addition, she wanted to get away from her parents, who tried to control her every movement, charged her for room, board, and utilities, and disapproved of her attempts at Americanization. My father was also feeling the pressures of age. He was almost thirty. At his age, my paternal grandfather had already fathered three children, including my father. My parents both felt the other was a perfect choice of mate. Both were recent Italian immigrants of the Roman Catholic faith. They held many of the same views about child rearing. My father also found it attractive that my mother was nearly fluent in English, a trait he lacked but felt was necessary for his children to be successful in this land of opportunity.

My parents wanted to start a family immediately. A year later, my older sister, Josephine, was born. I followed two years later. During this period, both my parents worked. My mother continued to work as a seamstress until the seventh month of each pregnancy. They saved as much as they could, and six months after I was born, they were able to purchase a house of their own in Bensonhurst. They both continued to work, leaving my maternal grandmother to take care of Josephine and me.

As we grew, it became difficult, especially in my case, to determine which language I should speak. During the day, my grandmother spoke Italian to us in a "Barese" dialect. At night, my mother spoke English to us and my father broken English and Italian in a Sicilian dialect. According to my parents, when I was first learning to speak, I would often combine the different languages. Josephine could speak both English and Italian; when she was younger, my mother spoke Italian to her. As a result, she had some trouble learning English but eventually learned both. This is why my mother decided to speak only English with me. My mother instructed my grandmother to communicate to me in English through Josephine, who was also told only to speak English to me. In effect, I lost much of my ability to speak Italian, but learned English very well. This became apparent in elementary school, where many of the children were brought up speaking both Italian and English, or in some cases only Italian, and had difficulty learning in a totally English environment. I could not understand this difficulty.

When I was four and Josephine six, my parents purchased a second home. The first was too small, for my sister and I had to share a bedroom. My parents kept the first house as a source of income and because my maternal grandmother (my grandfather had died of cancer when I was two) chose to remain there. This second house was a block away from the first. During the week, Josephine and I lived with our grandmother. This was because both parents chose to work full time. This continued until I was seven, when my mother became pregnant again with my younger sister, Maria.

During this time, my father had become an excellent mechanic. He tried owning his own business, but found he could not deal with his employees, many of whom were also immigrants. This is ironic considering his position when he first came to America. He gave up owning his own business and has worked for various foreign car dealerships in New York City for a number of years. My mother remained a seamstress, helping the family by providing a second income. She stopped working in factories when Maria was born because she wanted to be able to take care of her children. Thirteen months later, my youngest sibling, Anthony, was born. Even while raising young children, she continued to work as a seamstress, doing piecework at home for a local factory.

My parents' method of raising children differed for the older and younger pairs. In the case of my older sister and me, my parents were extremely strict. They kept a close eye on our education and made sure we did our schoolwork well. We were given very few privileges and were discouraged from having friends. As a result, I have become very shy and have a hard time meeting new people. My parents tried to raise us the way they were brought up in Italy, with total respect and obedience for the parents, and little if any control over our own lives. My mother, who herself had been trying to become more assertive and free when she came to America, was heavily influenced by my father's much more traditional views. Both parents stressed education and hard work, but forgot that the purpose of this is to enjoy life more. As my sister and I grew older, we began to indicate that we wanted to enjoy life, as well as work hard and be successful. Our efforts have worn them down and made them less strict on Anthony and Maria.

There are still many conflicts between my parents and my siblings and me. When my sister was dating before marriage, my parents felt she should not be alone with her boyfriend, but should have a traditional courtship much like their own. Another problem has arisen in raising Anthony and Maria. Both parents work constantly and do not recognize the need to spend time with their children. In Italy, no one ever made time for them, so why should they act differently? Josephine and I were not really bothered by this, but for Anthony especially, the need to spend time with his father is great. My mother makes time when she can, but my father, in his narrow traditional views, fails to recognize Anthony's need for his father. These are examples of the conflicts between their old-world views and our Americanized ones.

My parents, despite their faults, have done well in this country. They own two homes. Their two older children are doing well in their pursuit of higher education. The younger ones show promise of doing just as well. My father is a successful auto mechanic. My mother enjoys working and being a housewife. My father still clings to many of his traditional views, while my mother considers herself very American. Overall, though, they have been very successful and fortunate here in America.

Lizette Aguilar (SUNY Binghamton 1994)

Getting to Know My Parents So That I May Know Who I Am

It's about 5:30 P.M., two days after Thanksgiving. I am at my father's house in Paterson, New Jersey, having my second Thanksgiving dinner. My parents are divorced so every year I celebrate two Thanksgivings, two Christmases, etc., etc.

I am the daughter of a black Peruvian and a white Puerto Rican. I choose to put the color of my parents' skin before their nationality because in this country that is how they are seen: first by the color of their skin and then by their country of origin. My essay focuses mostly on my father's life and his experience as an immigrant in this country since he was affected more by the ways of this country. I briefly discuss my mother's life and her experience as an immigrant.

My father, Jose Aguilar, was born in Lima, Peru, on October 22, 1948. His father, Francisco Aguilar, was a successful construction worker and foreman, and his mother, Katalina Margarita Cartajena de Aguilar, was a housewife. They had ten children, five girls and five boys. They were all born and raised in Lima, Peru. Lima is the capital of Peru and is located on the coast. It has approximately 3.5 million inhabitants.

My father's life in Peru was simple until his father died when he was thirteen years old. His father's occupation as a construction worker–foreman allowed them to live a middle-class life, but with him gone, my father had to work by day to help support the family and attend school at night. He worked in a clothing factory making underclothes.

My father, who was very good in school, became less interested when he began to work. He began to fall behind, and before he knew it his younger brother, Alfredo, was catching up to him academically. My father felt that his younger brother was sure to pass him. This was a problem because my father's family stressed academic achievement and the children were expected to excel in school. My uncle's success made my father feel as if he had to prove himself to the family. By the eleventh grade, my father stopped going to school, and at the age of nineteen he decided to come to the United States. He left for two reasons: he wanted to help out more with the family income and he felt that at least his family would now be able to say, "Well, Alfredo is a doctor, and Jose, he lives abroad." All of his brothers and sisters did their best to convince him to change his mind but it was to no avail; my father was headstrong and stubborn. He looked to his older brother, Juan Francisco, who was an engineer, for financial help. Juan Francisco also made an effort to change my father's mind. He told my father about the racism that he might encounter in this country, but my father was determined to go, and so he did.

At the age of twenty he packed his bags and headed to the United States. The last thing his older brother told him before he left was, "Remember if you leave here with the head of a lion don't come back with the tail of a mouse."

When my father left Peru, Gen. Juan Velasco Alvarado was in power. Gen. Juan Velasco began to nationalize all of the big industries. With the nationalization of big industries came inflation and the loss of jobs, but still one could manage to subsist in Peru. Until 1975 Peru was still one of the best countries to live in as far as economics were concerned. My father said that his decision to leave Peru was not influenced by the political situation in his country at the time.

My father arrived in this country with only fifty dollars in his pocket. He would soon learn that what his older brother told him was true. But there was a tradition among his friends that helped him in his adjustment. After he was in the United States two weeks, his friends sent his return plane ticket back to Peru, because they knew that after two months in this country he would probably want to go back. Without that ticket, my father was forced to cope with his experiences here.

After his arrival, my father stayed with a friend in New Jersey and took a job cleaning jewelry. Within months of being in the United States my father was able to afford to live in a room of his own. His friend knew of an Italian family that was renting a room. My father's friend spoke to the family and made arrangements for my dad to see the room. When they arrived, my father's friend introduced my father to the wife. When she saw that my father was black she immediately said that the room was rented out and slammed the door in his face. This was my father's first racist experience, but it was not the last. He realized that in this country to be black, whether you were African American or South American, was to be without opportunities. Knowing this, he married my mother who was a white Puerto Rican.

My mother, Antonia Aguilar, was born in Cebradilla, Puerto Rico, but her birth certificate states that she was born in Isabella, Puerto Rico. Her mother is Matilde Perez and her father Rafael Gonzalez. Like many Puerto Ricans they left Puerto Rico because their economic situation was at poverty level. My grandmother was a housewife and my grandfather was a self-employed mechanic. Because my grandfather was self-employed, my mother grew up moving around a great deal until she was eleven years old. Finally, her family settled down in San Tulce, Puerto Rico. She lived in the projects of San Tulce from the age of thirteen.

Her parents immigrated in 1964, thinking that there would be more job opportunities in the United States. Instead, they found themselves living under conditions similar to those in Puerto Rico. Since both of my grandparents were uneducated, the family received public assistance. My mother, who was sixteen years old at the time her parents moved to the United States, was forced to terminate her education in the middle of her senior year of high school and go to work. My mother and her older sister, Ana, were sent to work in a sewing factory. My mother was never able to finish her education because she started a family very early.

When I spoke to my mother about her migration experience she didn't seem to have been too affected by the different society that she now lives in. This was probably due to two reasons. First, my mother looks white and probably did not encounter any racism from white Americans. (However, my mother has mentioned that she encountered prejudice from African Americans.) Second, she had a very difficult family life and tries to forget a lot concerning those years that she lived with her parents.

My father, however, had a different story. In the United States he dealt with racism for the first time. While doing the interview, I remembered something that my father had said to me when I was fifteen. He had just discovered that I had a boyfriend and was quite upset. He was upset, first, because I had a boyfriend, and second, because he was black. When my father told me he didn't want me with a black person I couldn't comprehend. I couldn't understand why someone who is black himself could not like someone else because they were black. So I asked him why he felt this way and he proceeded to answer. He said that it wasn't that he hated black people but instead that he didn't want me to have children with a black

Lizette Aguilar and her mother, Antonia, ca. 1977, Bronx, New York.

person because "unfortunately, in this country, black people have no opportunities. It is not that I hate them because as you can see my whole family in Peru is black, but in Peru things are different. You do not get treated differently for being black. Don't get me wrong, racism and prejudice exist everywhere, but in Peru it is not to the extent that it occurs in the U.S." He went on to tell me that it wasn't until he came to this country that he realized that he was black. This was the reason he married my mother. He felt that if his children were lighter than he then they would have a better chance at succeeding.

From interviewing my parents, I realize that they only integrated into American society because they needed to survive in this country. In my eyes, my mother didn't assimilate because she has taught us her culture and stresses that we never forget it. My father rejects assimilation because he feels that American culture is too superficial, too fast, and doesn't have a strong moral foundation. He feels that it is superficial because people are ruled by the dollar to the point passed by necessity. He feels it is too fast because children are exposed to adult issues and adult situations early in life. And he feels it has a weak moral foundation because of the crime rate, the teenage pregnancy rate, and the overwhelmingly high divorce rate.

For me the word assimilation has a negative meaning. For me it means to sell out to a culture that is not your own and so to deny your true family heritage. I am very proud that my parents did not assimilate into American culture because then I wouldn't be the person I am today. I wouldn't have the strong cultural base that I benefit from today. By knowing where my parents came from, I am able to point the way to where I am going because I have role models and tangible evidence that I can be somebody. I feel that many Latinos do not succeed because of that lack of exposure to role models they can relate to. It makes me sad when I see that someone is Latino but fails to acknowledge that because they, or their parents, want them to assimilate into American culture.

Ann Fenech (SUNY Binghamton 1990)

Finding Home

The sun was setting as I sat with my parents at the kitchen table. My mother was drinking a mug of tea, resting her feet on one of the legs of my father's chair. My father, in an undershirt and plaid pants, was finishing a plate of spaghetti. From time to time, my two younger sisters would come into the room to listen for a while to my parents, who were speaking about their ethnic roots and their experiences of immigrating to America.

My mother began first, needing only a few questions to get her started on her story. She was born during World War II in the Philippines. The Japanese were occupying their village of Bulan at the time, so my mother was born in a barrio to which her family had fled. A year later, when the area was safer, they returned to Bulan.

Bulan was a port town in which most people made their living through fishing or farming. The biggest town event each year was a fiesta in May in honor of their patron saint. The fiesta activities included dances in the plaza, a fair, a beauty contest to choose "Miss Bulan," and a market where peddlers from all over the area sold their wares.

My mother lived with her grandfather, parents, three brothers, and two sisters. Their ethnicity was Malay and Spanish. The most famous member of my family tree is my great-great-grandfather Don Julian Gerona, who was a lawyer, a political leader, and a revolutionary during Spanish rule and early American occupation of the Philippines. According to my grandfather, the Americans considered him a resistance leader and had him deported to Guam. Today, he is mentioned in Philippine history books.

American culture, which had been introduced when the Philippines became a possession of the United States, was evident even in this small town of ten thousand people. Though the family spoke the Bikul dialect at home, they were educated in the English language at school. My grandparents named my mother after Eleanor Roosevelt, and today the letters that members of my mother's family send to each other are written in English.

My grandfather supported the family working as a teacher. The family also raised a few farm animals and rented small plots of land to tenant farmers. They probably would have been considered poor by America's standards, but my mother remembers her early years as being relatively carefree.

At sixteen, my mother left home to go to the University of Santo Thomas, in Manila, to study to become a nurse. While at the university, my mother decided she wanted to go to America. The main reason was for the economic opportunities; salaries for nurses in America were much higher than in the Philippines. The quota system for Asians had recently opened up and with the nursing shortage in America, Filipino nurses were being recruited to work. When I asked my mother if she had any reservations, since a few years earlier the quota for Asian immigration was zero, she said, "I didn't think about it because the idea of discrimination was completely foreign to me. The only discrimination I ever knew before was class differences between the rich and the poor."

Another factor in her decision was that many of her classmates in nursing school had already left for America. After two years of waiting for an immigration visa for permanent residence and despite her parents' desire for her not to leave home, my mother immigrated to America in November 1966, sponsored by the Jewish Hospital of Brooklyn. My mother was grateful that the wait to immigrate was only two years. When she came to America, she started procedures to bring over her younger sister. Her sister had to wait fifteen years to immigrate. "In the Philippines, everyone wants to come to America. There's a long line," said my mother.

My mother came with fifty dollars in her pocket and a second cousin as her only relative in America. Her plan was to come to America, with the option to go back to the Philippines if she did not like American life. She found, despite some different customs, such as American supermarkets that did not exist at the time she lived in the Philippines, adjustment was not too hard because she had a nonchalant attitude and tried to take things in stride. Also, my mother's closest friends were other recent Filipino immigrants, who provided a support system.

A couple of years later, on a bus tour of the fall foliage of the Finger

Lakes, my mother met my father who was a recent immigrant from Tunisia. Six months later, they married.

At this point of my mother's story, my father had finished his dinner, and I asked him to fill in the story of his immigration experience. My father's parents had migrated to the United States and lived there briefly, but left before they became citizens. Years later, my father came back to America as an immigrant himself. My grandmother was from Bavaria, Germany. Her father had died when she was young and her mother worked to support a large family by farming and being the town midwife. After World War I, the area of the country where my grandmother lived was devastated and there were limited future economic prospects for her since the family farm was going to an older sister.

At the age of sixteen, my grandmother came to America, her passage paid by an older sister who lived in Queens, New York. My grandmother found work with a wealthy German American family who hired her as a governess to teach German to their children. She lived with the family in New York and later in China. A few years later, she moved back with them to America and met my grandfather, an immigrant to the United States from Malta.

My grandfather was born in Malta near the turn of the century. When he was young, his father was making a voyage to Australia as a merchant sailor, but the ship never came back, perhaps sunk in a wreck. To feed her children, his mother spent her days at the docks, loading bags of flour onto ships. My grandfather was often left by himself and instead of going to school, as his mother desired, he skipped school and got involved with a neighborhood gang, never learning to read or write. According to my father, the gang asked my grandfather to commit a murder. He refused and, fearing for his life, said a quick goodbye to his family and signed on a merchant ship as a sailor. He stayed with the ship for a few years, traveling all over the world. When his ship docked in Brooklyn, New York, he jumped ship. He was tired of traveling and he liked America well enough.

In America, my grandfather worked many odd jobs, as an electrician and painter. He married my grandmother, and their oldest son, Frank, was born in the United States. My grandfather was making a success for himself in America. He briefly owned a pet shop and later a grocery store. However, my grandfather was getting sicker and sicker from rheumatic heart disease. The doctor told him it was necessary to change climates and move to a place where it was warmer. My grandparents decided to move to Tunisia because my grandfather had family there and because it was close to Malta. If it were not for my grandfather's sickness, my father said

Wedding portrait, Gaetan Fenech and Anna Borst, October 20, 1928.

Gaetan Fenech (left), in front of his grocery store in Brooklyn, ca. 1930.

the family would have stayed in America. My grandparents owned a successful business and both had started procedures to become naturalized.

My grandparents moved to La Goulette, a port city in Tunisia, where my father was born. There, my grandfather was also successful. At one point, he owned three stores and furnished ships with the items necessary for their trips. However, my grandfather's sickness forced him to give up his stores and open a bazaar instead. When my father was four, my grandfather died, and my uncle quit school at the age of thirteen to run the store and support the family.

My father was able to remain in school and earn what would be equivalent to a high school diploma. Though his family spoke English among themselves, my father was educated in the French language at school because at the time Tunisia was a French protectorate. My father also learned Arabic and Italian to communicate with the shoppers who came into his store.

My father remembers life in Tunisia as being very difficult. He worked at the store immediately after school until closing and never had time for friends or social activities. He says he always felt like a foreigner in Tunisia although he was born there. His family was Catholic and of European descent, and they felt out of place in an overwhelmingly Arabic and Muslim culture.

When my father was eighteen, my uncle married a French teacher and moved to France. My father took over the store and started taking correspondence courses in accounting. Times in Tunisia were changing, however. The country had gained its independence from France, and in an effort to build nationalism, the government was passing laws to prevent Europeans from staying in Tunisia. At that time, one could not be a citizen unless both parents were already Tunisian citizens. Thus my father was never considered a Tunisian citizen although he had been born and raised there. Furthermore, he had no hope of ever becoming a citizen.

When my father was in his early twenties, Tunisia passed a law barring foreigners from owning businesses. My father had to close down his shop, but because the economy was so bad, he could not find a buyer. He got a job in the Pakistani Embassy in Tunisia as an English-French translator and, along with my grandmother, began to make plans to emigrate. My father says he felt he had no choice but to follow the growing exodus of other Europeans from the country. Labeled a foreigner, he was discriminated against. He knew there would never be any economic opportunities for him in a country where he said he was a "second-class citizen."

My father said that his attempt to leave the country was the worst pe-

ATLANTIQUE - ÉPICERIE

G. FENECH

18, Rue Cardinal Lavigerie — LA GOULETTE

Fournitures Militaires

Marchandises de 1er Choix

PRIX DÉFIANT TOUTE CONCURRENCE

FOURNITURES POUR LA MARINE

MAISON DE CONFIANCE

TÉLÉPH. 54

Business card of Gaetan Fenech, La Goulette, Tunisia, ca. 1932. He sold military furnishings and naval goods.

riod of his life. Having a country to live in is something most people, especially Americans, take for granted. My father, however, faced a series of rejections as he attempted to find a new home. Though a Maltese citizen, Maltese officials would not let my father immigrate there unless he had been born in the country. He faced similar restrictions blocking his entrance into France, Great Britain, or Germany.

Finally, my grandmother moved back to America, sponsored again by her sister and, in turn, my grandmother sponsored my father. At the age of thirty, in 1968, my father closed the doors of his house in Tunisia for the last time and left for New York. My father says he was insecure about coming to America because he was leaving the only home he had known, and he had to make a new life for himself. He also knew that if things did not work out in America, there would be no turning back because he would never be allowed to return to Tunisia.

In America, he married my mother, had three children, and has worked as an accountant. As soon as they could, my parents became U.S. citizens. I think they have both assimilated into American culture as much as immigrants can. We speak English at home and, except for a strict Catholic upbringing, my parents have not passed on to my sisters and me any of the traditions of their homelands.

My father said he feels like he did not have a native land. I think that because father was so acutely aware of being an outsider in Tunisia he was sensitive about his children ever having the same feeling. My mother said she never felt close enough to her Filipino heritage to pass it on, and she did not want her children to feel different; she wanted them to be Americans. I'm not sure if I have missed out on something because I am not familiar with either the language and customs of my heritage.

Since my parents have tried so hard to assimilate, it has not been difficult for my sisters and me to be the daughters of immigrants. I remember in second grade, I was very upset when a classmate made fun of my mother's Asian ethnicity, but besides that, I don't think I have ever been treated differently.

Though my family roots cover many countries, America is the only country I feel a connection to. For my parents and their children, America is home.

Soo Y. Kim (SUNY Binghamton 1992)

The Assimilation Problems of My Family in America

I have often asked my parents the reasons behind our immigration to the United States, but they have always been ambiguous in their answers. My father would give different reasons on different occasions, depending on his mood. One day he would declare better education for his children as a motive but a few days later he would alter it to military and political instability. I can remember about half a dozen motives my father has given me for our departure from South Korea to the United States.

My father first heard of America when he was in grade school in the early 1940s. Back then Japan had colonized Korea and had attempted to efface Korean culture and replace it with Japanese culture. Korean teachers were replaced by Japanese. Koreans were forced to adopt Japanese names, and Koreans were also forbidden to speak their native tongue in school. My father was also taught by the Japanese that America was an enemy and that he was to hate America and all its allies. But because Japan was hated by most Koreans for its brutal occupation, most Koreans, including my father, never believed Japan's propaganda that was aimed at execrating the United States.

My father was twelve years old when the Korean War broke out in 1950. By then he had already lost both of his parents and was living with his five siblings. As the war progressed, the North Korean Communists threatened to advance down toward Seoul, the capital of South Korea, where my father was living. Most Koreans in that area, including my father and his siblings, evacuated, journeying down toward the southern part of Korea. Amidst the chaos of the evacuation, my father and his siblings became separated, none of them knowing where the others were.

Even though my father was an orphan who had lost contact with all his siblings, he was fortunate enough to be taken in by an American doctor, Captain Montgomery, who provided him with food, shelter, and encouragement to pursue his education. In return, my father worked as a houseboy at the U.S. Army Hospital at the tender age of fourteen.

To my father, the captain was an embodiment of the paternalistic United States. He longed to go to America, which was to him the land of hope, of the free and the rich. To an orphan boy, America was the only ticket out of the poverty- and war-stricken country. So when the captain expressed his desire to adopt him and send him to Dallas, Texas, my father jumped at the chance.

When my uncles finally found my father after a long search and heard of his decision to move to America with the captain, they refused to sign the papers that were needed to finalize the adoption procedure. My father's sister-in-law tried to talk him out of it, telling him that his home was in Korea, where his siblings were. Feeling tremendous guilt, my father declined to go to America with the captain.

After the war, and throughout his college years, my father worked as a cargo checker at an American army depot in Seoul. Even though jobs were scarce after the war, my father's knowledge of some English, which he picked up while living with the captain, helped him get the job at the depot.

My father never stopped dreaming of going to America. When he was in his early twenties he immersed himself in American culture, emulating Americans by wearing American clothing and watching American movies. His "Americanization" started during this time, well before our immigration to the United States. For instance, when my father was courting my mother in the late 1950s, he behaved in a way that was more acceptable in America, such as smooching in public, just as he had seen in American movies. Public display of affection was not accepted in Korea during that time.

My parents married in 1960 and had three children, one son and two daughters. They slowly built a life for themselves and their children, and by the time of our immigration in 1979, our family had reached the status of upper middle class in Korean society. We had a very comfortable life in Korea. Our family was able to afford a two-story house, a housekeeper, and a garden full of red roses. But despite these luxuries, my parents never felt a sense of security after the division of Korea in 1953. My parents told

Kim family portrait, South Korea, 1970. Soo Youn is sitting on her father's lap.

me that they lived in constant fear of a second Korean War. For example, whenever there was a loud explosion from a construction site nearby, my parents could not eat, for the explosion reminded them of the bombs of the Korean War.

My father also told me that President Park, an authoritarian leader who had ruled South Korea with an iron fist from 1961 until his assassination in 1979, manipulated people's feelings toward North Korea. Park used people's fear of a second Korean War in his propaganda to unite the South Koreans under his leadership. In the media as well as in schools, South Koreans were taught to hate the North Koreans and to unite to fight Communism.

There were other reasons why my father wanted to leave South Korea. Prospects for good education and careers were dim for his children due to high competition resulting from a population explosion after the Korean War in South Korea. There was political instability due to anti-Park activities on the part of college students. Many of those college students were persecuted, and political freedom did not exist in the country.

My father finally decided to immigrate to America in 1976 just after my brother returned from a weekend of army training, which was required of all male high school students. When my father saw my brother sunburned and exhausted, scenes from the Korean War flashed before his eyes. He remembered the suffering and the starvation of the war. He was also afraid that his only son would serve in the army of a country that might go to war at any time.

My mother never wanted to come to America, even though she heard that it was a place of opportunity and wealth. Because of the Korean War, my mother also thought of the Americans as the protectors of Koreans. She remembered the American soldiers who had brought chocolate, gum, and candies to starving Korean children and she rejoiced, thinking how wonderful America was. But her mother and her siblings were in Korea, and she never thought of leaving them. But after my father's endless demands to leave Korea, my mother finally complied with his wishes, just as Korean society expected a dutiful and loyal wife to do.

Our family arrived in Queens, New York, in 1979. The immigration to the United States was a step down the social ladder for our family. We moved into a small apartment with no furniture and both my parents looked for work, finding only low-paying jobs open to them. My father worked at a clothing store, and my mother found a job as a seamstress in a clothing factory.

Our immigration was particularly hard on my mother. She was forced to go to work because our income was low and also because my father did not want her to be idle. She did not know any English, and her life in America was not like what she was accustomed to. When my mother was growing up in Korea, she was raised to become a housewife, like most women of her generation. Most women were educated until their high school years, concentrating their studies on home economics and learning how to be good wives and mothers. She was a typical, traditional Korean woman in that she learned to become dependent on her husband and her family.

She tried to assimilate into American culture by learning English first. But working a ten-hour shift and raising a family deterred her efforts, and she only became frustrated. My mother has not assimilated much because her life is surrounded by everything Korean. She only associates with Koreans at work, and when she comes home, she only watches Korean programs on TV. She feels comfortable living in our neighborhood where there is a large population of Koreans, and whenever my father talks of moving to a white neighborhood, my mother refuses vehemently. My mother still does not speak English.

My father thinks that his assimilation into American culture has been rather easy, facilitated by his employment by the U.S. Army in Korea. He accepts most aspects of American culture but has been shocked by the treatment of the elders in America. Elders in Korea are put on a pedestal and respected by young people. This tradition stems from the influence of Confucianism, which promotes ancestor worship. Even in modern Korea, the best seats on buses and trains are specifically reserved for the elderly. My father thinks that Americans have no respect for elders, for he has witnessed parent abuse and "granny dumping," which is the abandonment of one's elderly parents. He feels that Americans are too individualistic and have no loyalty toward family members.

He also was shocked by the prevalent racism in America. When he was working for the U.S. Army in Korea, he witnessed intermingling of people of all colors, which led him to believe that racism did not exist in America. But here he witnessed blatant as well as subtle racism, especially at his work, where he feels that certain groups are favored by the supervisors.

My father has slowly changed his role as a strict traditional Korean father into a more lenient, "Americanized" father. He never used to go into the kitchen, for he believed it was not a proper thing for a man to do. Now he has become more domesticated, washing dishes and even cooking once in a while.

He did not allow my older sister to go away to college or to stay out late at night, for he thought that a young woman should stay home as much as possible, and to do otherwise would ruin her reputation. But by the time I had reached eighteen, my father allowed me to have the freedom to choose any college I wanted to attend and to stay out late at night.

Even though my father feels that he has assimilated into American culture, he associates exclusively with other Korean men of his generation. He participates in his high school and college alumni associations, attends prefectural associations and *gye,* a Korean equivalent of the rotating credit association. These associations serve as an outlet for the anxiety and frustrations my father feels as an immigrant. It also gives him a place to go where he can reminisce and relate to others who have lived through the hardships of the Japanese Occupation and the Korean War.

Both of my parents often think of returning to Korea and wish to be buried in their motherland. But they feel torn between returning to Korea and remaining here because their children and grandchild have already made their lives in America. For now they plan to stay in America to watch their children become successful.

My older sister was almost sixteen years old when we immigrated to America. When we first arrived, she experienced culture shock and did not know how to react. She just followed my parents' orders to attend school and to return home. When comparing American and Korean culture, my older sister prefers the American lifestyle. Unlike my father, she likes the individualistic aspect of American culture because she feels that, in Korean culture, family may limit one's freedom to choose a lifestyle. In Korea, children are supposed to conform to their parents' wishes in choosing their schools and careers. Korean women are not expected to stay out late at night and are not supposed to date any men, except a future marriage partner. She feels that Korean parents are too strict, not caring for their children's desires and only teaching their children to obey them.

My sister, too, has felt subtle racism at her work. Whenever she is doing business over the phone, she feels that her Korean accent hinders her business transactions for people on the other line treat her as a foreigner.

My sister feels torn between the two cultures. For example, as she was preparing for her marriage, her fiancé asked her to give up her career and to become a housewife. In Korea, the wife of a first son usually stays home and takes care of his parents. Since my sister's fiancé was a first son, he asked her to become that traditional wife. My sister was also pressured by our parents to comply to that tradition for it was the "proper" thing for a Korean woman to do. My sister had always dreamed of becoming a successful career woman but she also wanted to get married and have a family of her own. For months she was in a dilemma, not knowing whether she should break off the engagement or not. Fortunately, her fiancé's mother gave permission for him and my sister to lead an independent life, and for her to do whatever she wants.

My initial experience in America was rather positive. When I first entered American school in the third grade, my teacher and most students treated me like a special guest at their school. They went out of their way to be nice and helped me to learn English.

The students who made me feel unwelcome were other Korean students who spoke fluent English. They were reluctant to translate for me and made me feel like an F.O.B. (fresh off the boat) or greenhorn. Thus, I became friends with other newly arrived immigrants who spoke very little English.

I overcame the frustrating experience of learning English rather quickly in elementary school because I befriended a newly arrived Rumanian girl. Even though neither of us spoke much English we communicated by using hand and foot gestures, and we encouraged each other to learn English. I think that if I had limited my friends to Korean Americans, I would have become dependent on their translations, which would have only hindered my learning of English.

My fluency in English, which came at the expense of developing my Korean language skills, has become a barrier between my parents and me. I have a hard time communicating with my parents because I have forgotten many Korean words to express my feelings. There are times when I have to use a Korean English dictionary to convey my thoughts to my parents. Sometimes my older sister acts as a translator for us.

It has been almost thirteen years since my family immigrated to America, and I have always considered myself to be an American. Yet I still feel like a stranger in this land. When I go out, especially in rural areas, I am stared at like a circus freak and people ask me what country I am from. I have been called "Chink" many times and have witnessed hostility toward Asian Americans, who are treated as a threat to other Americans, or as the "Yellow Peril."

As I grew older, I unconsciously sought out the friendship of other Asian Americans, especially Korean Americans. It became harder for me to relate to my non-Asian friends who just did not understand Korean parents' expectations and the Korean culture that was embedded in me. I felt as if I had to offer justifications for my thoughts and actions, and in return all I would get from others were blank stares. However, my Asian American friends understand the pain of encountering racism and the problems of assimilation that we have all experienced.

Soo Youn Kim (second from right) and fellow Binghamton graduates, 1994.

I also think there is a difference in socialization of Asians and non-Asians. I have been taught not to be too intrusive or revealing of my personal life. Thus I am too reserved to be accepted by many non-Asian Americans and at times I feel out of place with them. Sometimes I do not know how to act in front of the parents of my non-Asian friends. When I am in the presence of a Korean elder, all I have to do is bow at them and keep quiet, and they will think that I am a polite person. But whenever I meet the parents of my non-Asian friends I am uncertain as to how I should behave in front of them.

If I went back to Korea, I would also stick out like a sore thumb. Korean women of my age are expected to prepare for marriage, and women who are career-oriented, as I am, are a rarity. Korea is much more of a patriarchal society than is America, and the women's movement is practically unknown. As an Americanized woman, I would suffocate in Korea.

I have absorbed both Korean and American cultures, yet I do not feel I belong to either one—I do not feel that I fit into either society. I am neither Korean nor American, and yet I am both.

PART III

Ethnicity in Our Lives

The final group of essays offers views of the United States today, for it brings together the stories of students who were either born in this country in the 1960s or immigrated here in the 1970s or 1980s. These students came of age after the abolition of the national origins quota system, in a period in which Asian and Latin American immigrants predominated. They are a group—including four Asians, two blacks, and one Mexican American—who feel very keenly their differences from white, mainstream America.

These students have been challenged to come to terms with their multiple identities—as ethnics and as Americans, or as emigrants from another culture making lives for themselves in the United States. The titles of their essays resonate with this conflict: "Black on the Outside, White on the Inside"; "Being Indian in America"; "Triple Identity."

Two of the students—Jaime Dominguez from Los Angeles and Lila Shah from Syracuse—recall periods in their lives when they tried to be two very distinct people, well-adjusted "Americans" out in the public, and Mexican and Indian, respectively, within their immediate families. Neither Jaime nor Lila could maintain this schizophrenic existence very long. Both overcame the need to fit into their teenage peer group and accepted the value of their family's cultural traditions. They came to accept their differences from other Americans and to see the value of those differences for the larger society. In a similar way, Puwat Charukamnoetkanok came to appreciate his triple identity and to draw upon Chinese, Thai, and American cultures as he constructed his own identity in this country. All three emphasize the freedom that they derive from their multiple identities and from having the strength to become their own selves without regard to peer or community pressures.

The articulation in these accounts of the possibility of maintaining hybrid identities—of being simultaneously Indian and American, or Thai, Chinese, and American—is evidence of a distinctly new set of ethnic possibilities in American society. Throughout the twentieth century the United States has been a multicultural society, but the character of that multiculturalism has changed, something we can see clearly in these essays. The families of European-born immigrants, as they are described by their grandchildren in the first section of this volume, experienced a relatively straightforward adoption of dominant American values over the course of the generations. In contrast, contemporary immigrants emphasize the possibility of maintaining multiple, and at times conflicting, cultural allegiances.

But even these new possibilities offer only a partial view of immigration today. Two of the students writing in this final section feel less strongly the competing pulls of their two cultures. As refugees from Vietnam and the Soviet Union, Anh-Dao Nguyen and Vladimir Sinayuk feel stronger gratitude toward the United States and are less torn between the Old and New Worlds than are their fellow recent immigrants. As they construct their life stories, they express the conviction that there was no future for themselves or their families in their home countries, and they view the United States as a welcome refuge and source of hope. As with the earlier groups of essays, the stories in this section reflect the diversity of the pool of immigrants and refugees who came to the United States in the same period. There is no single overarching script that synthesizes their diverse experiences.

Cathy Thompson (UC San Diego 1988)

The Oreo Cookie: Black on the Outside, White on the Inside

My ethnic background is something that has caused me to constantly reflect on myself and my place in society. I am half "white" and half "black." My father was from Kenya, Africa, and my mother is American. My mother is a mixture of Dutch, English, Welsh, Irish, Spanish, French, and Indian. So I guess I am what some would call a mulatto.

Being of mixed blood has caused me much confusion throughout my life. My mom says that I am a white girl in a black body growing up in a white world. This is because I have had absolutely no contact with my natural father. My mother has raised me and has taught me her values and beliefs. In addition, the person I knew as my "daddy" for a good portion of my life was white. I did most of my growing and learning in white middle-class neighborhoods where my ethnicity was seldom understood. As a child I was somewhat confused by the fact that all of my relatives were white and I was black, but my family never called attention to the color difference. As a result I believed that the world was colorless and there was no need to question the issue.

I did not have a problem with this situation until other people came into the picture and forced me to realize that I was different, very different. I had my first encounter with prejudice when I was about five years of age. I lived in San Lorenzo, which is a quaint little suburban area outside of San Francisco. It was a predominantly white neighborhood with a few Asians and Mexican Americans, and maybe one or two other blacks besides me. As I was walking home from the park one day, a white teenage boy peered over his backyard fence and started calling me names like "nigger" and "blackie." He said that they didn't want any niggers there and that I should go back to where I came from. I was so upset by this I just ran home crying to my mommy. I know that it was hard for her at the time because she had to console me and explain something to me that she did not really understand. I did not know what nigger meant, but I knew it was bad. It was at this time that I realized I was different. When people look at me they see a black girl. I have dark skin, dark eyes, and thick, coarse hair. I've been told that I have white features, whatever that means, but based on overall general appearance I am black.

In addition to prejudice, I faced ignorance and misunderstanding. Every one of my friends experienced a feeling of shock and disbelief when I brought them to my house to meet my mother. Their first question, "Why are you black and your mom white?" I would just say, "I don't know, I guess because God wanted it that way." Their response, "Well you know what? She can't be your mother—you are adopted." "No! I'm not!" "How do you know?" How did I know? I found myself asking for proof of my relationship with my mother. She took the time to show me my birth certificate and baby pictures, things that I was convinced she would not have if she was not my real mother. But there was always someone trying to lead me to believe otherwise. My friends always seemed to be trying to convince me that I was adopted. They told me that my mom could have changed my birth certificate, and that if she had adopted me as a baby, she would have baby pictures, anyway. Even though I believed my mother, there was a slight doubt lurking in the back of my mind for many, many years.

Throughout my life I have had to explain myself and defend my blood relationship to my mother. It was difficult because I, myself, did not really understand the particulars of how I came to be. For a long time I thought that I was a freak of nature or something. I believed that my father was that white man who lived with me between the ages of one and four and eight and twelve. He and my mother married before I was born, and I knew him as "daddy." After about the age of six my mom tried to explain to me that my natural father was black but I just could not grasp the concept. I figured she was talking about my "godfather," and that is what I told my friends. I was nine or ten years old before I realized that I was in no way related to Mr. Thompson. He introduced me to one of his friends saying, "This is my wife's daughter, Cathy." I was extremely hurt by this statement and the realization that our whole relationship had been a lie, but at least I finally knew the truth and was able to explain my situation to my friends.

By the time I was in fourth or fifth grade I understood and was proud of my ethnicity. I had no problem telling people that I was half black and half white. Most of my friends could accept this and there were no further difficulties. Just when I was finally learning to anticipate people's reactions to my background, I was faced with a strange and new phenomenon. I encountered prejudice not from whites (which I expected and could deal with), but from blacks, whom I thought were just like me. At the age of ten I came to San Diego and had my first real interaction with other blacks. Everything was fine until they met my mother. I explained that I was mixed and they called me "white-washed." They noticed differences in my personality, in my attitudes and values, and concluded that it was because of the fact that I was white. They also assumed that I thought I was somehow better than they were because I was not fully black. Actually, it was they who carried that notion, and I was totally disoriented by their nonacceptance of my heritage and of me. Well, it was only a matter of time before they realized that they were being stupid and we became friends, but this forced me to deal with a different aspect of prejudice and misunderstanding. I had thought that life would be easier because blacks would be more sympathetic to or understanding of my situation, but this was not the case. They scrutinized my personality and actions in an attempt to find differences or peculiarities.

It is hard for me to know and understand who or what I am. I have had a hard time identifying with blacks because I have spent most of my life with whites. It is very sad because many times I do not feel accepted by either group. I am not what most people, black or white, expect a black person to be. I do not sound black, either in accent or use of language. After all, I learned to talk from listening to my mother. I do not act black. I have different values and ambitions than most of the black people I know. The only thing black about me is my physical appearance. I have been raised in a white household, so for all intents and purposes I am white. After realizing this about me, people either totally reject me and assume that I think I am better because I am different, or they patronize me because they think so. There are very few instances where I am accepted for who and what I am. Some people even go so far as to try to teach me how to be more black, or they hang around with me hoping some of my whiteness will rub off.

My ethnic experience is quite different from that of other black Americans. I have a hard time relating to some of their attitudes because I have been raised in a totally different environment. Most blacks come from a family whose history parallels the "black history" we are learning. Their ancestors were slaves. Their grandparents had to ride in the back of the

Jaime Dominguez (UC San Diego 1988)

Should I or Shouldn't I?

Many unfortunate children are sometimes caught between asking themselves, "Who am I?" and "Why am I different?" Consequently, many youngsters have lost touch with their cultural heritage due to pressure of socialization in American society. As for myself, I was caught between the struggle of recognizing my Mexican descent and the importance of it to me. My family always pressured me to recognize the importance of keeping my Mexicano culture. I was caught between disassimilation and assimilation with the Anglo culture. Although the struggle swung back and forth, my educational maturity helped me to come closer to my culture in that I am now proud to say that I'm Mexicano.

A brief explanation of some of the terms used in this essay may be useful in better understanding the story. Here is a definition for each: *barrio*—the local neighborhood; *placazo*—graffiti of gang member names; homeboy/holmes—the barrio good friend; *raza*—Mexican people/culture; and Dogtown—name of the project and local gang. Such terms are slang that are used on a daily basis in our barrio.

Life has always been difficult, especially for my mother, Micaela Dominguez. My mother, who is of Indian descent through my grandmother's side, lived in the small town of Piatla, just outside the city of Puebla, Mexico. Micaela married Joel Martinez at the age of seventeen and through the years she gave birth to six lovely children. Around her early forties, disaster struck when her husband was murdered. She was left a widow, having to raise all six children on her own. Times became extremely difficult in that she could no longer support and feed her children. Due to economic instability, my mother decided to migrate to the United States in search of a more prosperous life for her children. Finally, in early November 1961, my mother began her immigration journey, leaving behind all of her children in Mexico with her then boyfriend, Elias Dominguez, who would later become my father. In late November 1961, my mother crossed into the United States with a three-day tourist passport.

After her arrival in the United States, my mother lived in Los Angeles. Here, she worked in a sewing machine factory at $1.00 per hour day and night, although the minimum wage was $1.25 at the time. On weekends, she worked cleaning houses because she still did not have enough money to support herself. Because times became too difficult for my mother, my father migrated one year later in 1962 in order to assist her economically to bring her children to the United States. After four years of hard labor, pain, suffering, and sleeping in garages, my mother was finally able to bring all of her six children across into America on July 1965 with legal "permissions." Because of financial instability when they all arrived, my family had to settle in a housing project in East L.A. known as Dogtown because it was cheap housing. This barrio is the place where the first generation of the Dominguez family was to be born and raised.

On March 15, 1968, a child known as Jaime Dominguez was born to Micaela and Elias Dominguez. Being the fifth-born of seven Dominguez children, I was always watched over and cared for by all ten of my elder brothers and sisters. Although I was one of the favorites as a kid, my family had no idea of the hassle and trouble I was going to give them about being Mexicano and the confusion of my cultural roots. My older brothers and sisters did not know how to speak English, due to their growing up in Mexico, so the language I learned to speak first was Spanish. Spanish was the only language spoken in our home and around our barrio, making it difficult to learn to speak English. Everywhere I went around the barrio, whether it was the corner store, the gas station, or the local supermarket, everyone seemed to communicate in Spanish. Even today, things remain the same in the barrio. It was not until the first grade, in September 1974, that I encountered the English language.

My first exposure to the English language occurred in a predominantly Anglo elementary school, Erwin Street School, located in the San Fernando Valley. I recall when most of my friends and I were on a full bus, frightened to be heading for this new world for the first time. Most of us were being sent to such a school because our parents believed that our education would be better in an Anglo school. When I stepped out of the bus for the first time, I was scared and nervous. As I looked around, I was realizing that this place would be my home during school for the next six years. I recall walking into my classroom, very fidgety, frightened at what I saw—all white kids nicely dressed looking at me as if I was some kind of alien that they did not want to touch or get near.

During my six years at Erwin Street School, I went through a lot of pressure and cultural retention that affected my family and myself. There were several times when the Anglo kids would exclude us (Mexicanos/Mexicanas) from school activities and games because they were afraid of our skin color. For example, once during lunch as I tried to sit next to a group of white kids, they wouldn't allow me because they said my skin color didn't belong with theirs. Also, while I would sit in class, they would call me names such as, "beaners, wetbacks, and dirty animals" and ask me questions like "Why are you here? You people don't belong here." Overall, the other students had the idea and impression that we were insignificant and inferior to them. There were times when I would return home from school and cry to my parents about why was it that the Anglo kids always put us down and never wanted to play or associate with us Mexicanos. Very importantly, my family always said to me in Spanish, "Jaime, you are just as good as anyone else and remember that the Mexicano in you will always keep you going!" They wanted to make sure that I remembered who I was.

After becoming fed up with the continuous discrimination and harassment of the Anglo kids, I decided that the only way to avoid such a problem and fit in with the whites was to assimilate into their system. After the fourth grade, I no longer wanted to be recognized as a Mexicano but as an American, and worst of all, I became hesitant about wanting to speak Spanish on a daily basis. By the fifth grade, due to the socialization of the institution, teachers, and friends, I became known as Jimmy, not Jaime anymore. As a result, because I really had no knowledge of what socialization and assimilation was doing to me, this slow change caused a stir with my family, friends, and the barrio.

As soon as my family became aware of what the socialization was doing to me, they were stunned. Because my brothers and sisters held strong Mexican family values, they put extreme pressure on me so that I would not lose touch with my cultural roots. They began speaking only in Spanish to me. Whenever I tried to speak English around the house, all they did was ignore me and say *¿Que dices?* meaning "What did you say?" and walk away from me. They even went so far as to dress me like a Mexican nationalist, complete with guaraches, a zarape, and Mexican-style shirts.

When I graduated from Erwin Street School, I took my Americanization attitude into Mt. Gleason Junior High, another predominantly Anglo school located in the valley.

While I was in junior high school, the struggle to keep my Mexican heritage continued as I became an outcast in the eyes of my raza. My attitude toward my culture had changed so much that I became more and more distant from my raza. Before I realized it, I was caught up in trying to live in a two-sided world in order to fit in with both sides. I lived in the Anglo world during school and in the East L.A. world in the barrio after school. Unfortunately, this lifestyle did not last long as it backfired in high school. I tried living this life because being Mexican in a "white" society just did not seem to work and vice versa. Here are some incidents that reflect this difficulty.

Whenever I returned back to the barrio coming from school, my homeboys would criticize my presence, mainly the way I had changed my style of dressing and the way I spoke due to the socialization and acculturation I was developing in the Anglo environment. They no longer considered me a homeboy. They accused me of being a "want-to-be white boy" and no longer wanted to associate with me. It saddened me because I no longer was able to kick it with the cholos. Therefore, they did not allow me to write my placazo on the walls anymore, thus terminating my membership in the gang Dogtown. Due to this, I soon realized that the only way to get back into the "barrio scene" was to be like them, so I did. Now, whenever I came home from school, I would change my clothes and slip into the barrio clothes: pendletons, black shoes, and black Dickies pants. I also had to speak lots of Spanish to the homeboys. On the other side of the picture, things were the same only reversed. For example, upon arriving at Mt. Gleason, I had to be sure that I was in my usual PCH pants, OP shirts, wearing my canvas Nikes. Also, I had to leave my Spanish at home bringing with me the English accent.

This lifestyle did not last long because by the end of my eighth grade year, my cultural perception slowly began to change as I grew closer to my cultural roots. I found that denying my own identity and culture in order to fit into another ethnic group was a form of cultural and personal suicide. I started to become more aware of my actions around the Anglo community. My desire to grow closer to my culture was due to the strong influence of my elder brother Raul. Mainly because he was the first member of our family to go on to college (UC Irvine), he succeeded in becoming a positive Mexican example in the barrio. I soon saw that my stereotypes of Mexicans were misconceptions. I understood that Mexicanos also had the capabilities and qualifications to go on into higher education just as anyone else. When my other brother Miguel entered college (UC Santa Cruz), my lingering doubt about Mexicans not being smart and capable enough to attend college disappeared. Everything that the white kids and teachers had said to me about Mexicans being too dumb and lazy, and not having the motivation and perseverance to do well in life was now just a fallacy. Although my attitude changed about Mexicanos achieving excellence in higher education, the struggle with my cultural retention continued on through the early years of high school.

Now that I was attending Lincoln High School in East L.A., with a predominantly Chicano-Latino population, things were quite different. I no longer had to live in the two-sided world, although I still continued to be called Jimmy. In high school, I had finally comprehended who I was and the importance of keeping my identity.

When I brought some of my Anglo habits into this predominantly Chicano-Latino school, things just did not work out. I began to experience communication problems. Whenever I tried speaking in the valley language ("hey dude, it's awesome"), the new friends that I had established made fun of me. They would say things like "You better get your language straight because your 'want-to-be-a-white-boy' vocabulary is not accepted here!" After hearing such criticism on a daily basis, I realized that my friends were sending me a message saying that I had better recognize where I was and with whom I was dealing. At basketball and football games and during nutrition and lunch, there seemed to be some hesitation and distance due to my presence. For example, once during a football game, my friends did not allow me to cheer with them because they accused me of being different, and they didn't want to get a bad image. They still felt my appearance and language were my way of denying my true identity of being a "Mexican." There even came a time when my good friend Carolina asked me, "Are you sure you know who you are?" After heavy thinking due to such a question, I began to feel that I just was not being myself. At this point, I began to feel guilty that I had just sold myself for nine years to another culture while at the same time denying my own.

With the help of my family, and friends like Carolina, I was finally able to recognize my cultural roots. Soon, I began speaking bilingually to my classmates and community while changing my name back to Jaime. When this change occurred, no longer was I an outcast in my community, but I was recognized as a strong sentimental Mexicano, fighting to keep his culture strong.

Keeping my culture and retaining my Mexican roots has been a struggle, but thanks to my friends and family, I did not become a *vendido,* or sell-out. Through the accumulation of my past ethnic experiences in my educational institutions, I was able to identify my culture. I learned a lot in that if people are going to accept another person into their group, then they must accept that person for what he or she is, not by what they want the person to be or do. A person should not have to change his or her identity and lifestyle in order to assimilate into another culture to please others. Even today, my parents still stress the importance of keeping the Mexican culture within our family. This is why whenever my brothers, sisters, nieces, and nephews go to my mother's house, they are only allowed to communicate in Spanish. For example, I have a nephew who refuses to speak Spanish in my mother's home, so whenever he speaks to her or us in English, we give him the same treatment that my family gave me seven years ago: ignore him and walk away until he communicates in Spanish. It is important that we all keep our heritage and family ties strong. The experiences of being discriminated against were enough to reinforce my identity among the Anglos and Mexicanos. I can strongly say that I am proud to be a Mexican. No one can take that away from me, and no one should try. Viva la raza!

Catherine Tagudin (UC San Diego 1983)

My Experience with Immigration/Assimilation in America

Upon my mother's decision, we left the Philippine Islands ten years ago to seek the many opportunities we heard America had to offer. She felt that the instability of the political and economic situation in the Philippines, triggered by President Marcos's martial law, offered little advancement for the individual as well as the family. Moreover, my father was unemployed during that period, leaving my mother to play the role of the family "breadwinner." My family situation was also somewhat unstable, because my parents did not relate well to each other. This gave my mother an even stronger incentive to leave the country. With plans to petition for the rest of the family in the future, my mother took me, for I was the youngest in the family, and left for the United States. It was quite easy for us to travel to America with little red tape, for my mother was a native-born U.S. citizen. Furthermore, we had relatives in San Diego who welcomed us to stay at their home while we settled down. Thus, my mother and I were not the first in our family to venture to America.

Immigrants from the paternal side of my family consisted of aunts and uncles who came to this country to work and to study. From the maternal side of the family were my grandparents who came to elope, find work, and to study. However, the latter returned to the Philippines because of the Great Depression in the 1930s. Despite the vast number of years between migrations (maternal—1920s; paternal—1950s; my mother and I—1973), the reasons for leaving the Philippines remained the same: All sought America's opportunities to better their lives. In this process, all experienced some assimilation into the American way of life. Of all the members in my family, it seems that I have experienced the highest degree of assimilation. From my experience, I can suggest that the younger one comes to America, the easier and earlier one assimilates into its society. Being the youngest to immigrate from my family, I had been "Americanized" almost 100 percent.

As a child, I believed the many glorious tales of America expressed by the Disney movies I watched, as well as those tales from letters written by relatives from abroad. In fact, I generalized it to be a land of happiness free from the hardships of life. One may compare my feelings upon coming to this country with the feelings of a child who is about to go to Disneyland for the first time. I pictured it to be a place where poverty was unknown, where begging in the streets was unknown, and a place where cleanliness and order were greatly stressed. All the unhappy sights I had encountered in the Old Country, I believed to be unheard of in America. Upon my arrival, I was amazed at the cleanliness and order that surrounded me. For example, I was surprised to learn that America had machines built especially to sweep its streets. I was amazed at the magnificent freeway systems, as well the bright reflectors that served as its lane dividers, and I stood in shock when I learned that common household pets possessed the luxuries of specially made canned goods and even brilliant, rhinestone-studded collars.

Americans were considered a different class, not only because of their way of living, but also because of their unique features. They looked different. Anyone with hair lighter than black and skin more fair than brown stood out from the crowd. Although it was known that the United States had a potpourri of nationalities, the terms "Americano" and "Americana" had different connotations. The picture that first came to mind with these terms was that of a Caucasian—not a native American Indian, not a Mexican American, not an African American. This influence may have come from the days of World War II, Gen. Douglas MacArthur and the GIs, Hollywood, and the media. Those with light hair, light eyes, and fair skin were considered the elite in the Philippines. Because of this, members of the upper class tried to stay away from the sun. On a sunny day, it was not surprising to find people strolling in the parks under the shade of their umbrellas. Most people with darker features were commonly associated with the lower-class field workers who spent much of their time in the sun. Imagine my shock, then, when I first saw the oil-laden sun worshippers on the beaches of San Diego. A tan is a status symbol according to San Diegans—a symbol of health and fitness. I thought these Americans must think of the farm workers back home as being very healthy.

American foreigners in the Philippines had been an unusual sight. My uncle from the United States had brought his blond-haired, blue-eyed wife for a visit to his homeland. Needless to say, the neighborhood was mystified by her presence. People would peek through the windows just to get a glimpse of her. Children would touch her hair and the brave ones plucked a strand to show their friends. We were all intrigued by the delightful "Americana."

I believed that Americans had luxurious lives, and I wanted very much to live in their world. But to be a part of this world, I needed to blend into the American way of life. I was first introduced to its people when I attended an American public elementary school. My attendance in American public schools was the major factor in my "Americanization."

In the Philippines, I attended a very strict private Catholic school. In this school, discipline, cleanliness, and academic advancement were greatly stressed. The transition from this school to the American public school was an academic and cultural shock. I was introduced to my third-grade class as "a new student who comes from the Philippines." Because I was a foreigner, I was often ostracized by my classmates because they had never met anyone from such a distant land. They often talked to me slowly as if I had never heard the English language; they frequently asked why I always came to school so neatly dressed; they asked why I behaved so properly; they asked strange questions like "Do you have televisions in the Philippines?" and they asked how I knew so much English. I was insulted at their preconceptions of the Philippines, but it was understandable, for Americans had always been stereotyped as an elite culture. I discovered that this was not so. The American teaching pace was much slower than in the Philippines; in fact, I was considered one of the gifted in the class. Therefore, I no longer considered myself a second-rate person among these American children. I learned that we all varied in our academic potential despite our ethnicity. I found that those children whose families stressed the importance of education were the ones who succeeded academically.

I had some trouble adjusting socially during my first few weeks in America. I was quieter than the rest of my classmates because my accent often made it difficult for them to understand me. I was also unfamiliar with the slang they used to communicate. Moreover, I was not used to the freedom these children possessed in school and in the classroom. In the Philippines, classrooms were used strictly as learning areas. Any misconduct or inappropriate behavior led to punishment. The school itself was surrounded by guards and gates. All those who entered needed special identification cards and all personal possessions were subject to search. Because of the unstable political situation, the school administrators were afraid of terrorists and bomb threats. Therefore, all were searched, including the kindergartners. In America, I enjoyed the freedom given to me, but I needed time to shed the strict, disciplined conditioning I experienced in the Philippines. In a few weeks I became used to the American school system, and gradually I began to socialize. Consequently, I felt relaxed in my new environment. I spent so much time in school and with my friends that I unconsciously became more and more "American," like my classmates. My accent soon disappeared, and in the period of two years I became so used to speaking English that Tagalog became my second language instead of my first. This process happened much without my awareness; thus I did not make a great effort to become "Americanized."

My experience was different from that of my parents. As an eight-year-old, my mind was a "clean slate." My opinions were not yet formed and my ways were not yet set. The flexibility of an open mind was an advantage over those who immigrated at a later age. As I grew up in my new environment, I was exposed to a variety of customs, cultures, languages, and religions. My relatives, having lived most of their lives under one set of customs in the Philippines, understandably had a harder time adjusting.

Assimilation, for the most part, was easy for me since it evolved at an inconspicuous pace. The only time I had encountered conflict with my "Americanization" was at the arrival of my sister, brother, and father. (I had convinced my mom that her situation with my father might improve in America, therefore, she also petitioned for him.) My newly arrived family was shocked to learn that I was no longer fluent in my native language. They thought I purposely ignored my language because I was ashamed to be a Filipino. This was certainly not true, but it was difficult for me to convince them that I was no longer fluent in Tagalog because of lack of practice. My mother often spoke to me in Tagalog, but I found it easier to express myself in English. My mother felt no objection to my fluent English.

Another conflict that developed in my family concerned the preservation of Filipino values. In cases of sibling rivalry, my father demanded that the younger child should listen to the elder and take his suggestion without any questioning. He felt that the elder would be wiser in making decisions for he had experienced life longer, thus, should know better than the younger. Being the youngest in the family, I had no authority over anyone's actions. I rebelled against this value for I felt indignity and unfairness. I told my father that this was a form of dictatorship where one had no voice. He repeatedly said to me that I had become too "Americanized," which implied I lacked discipline. In the Filipino tradition, one takes the order of the father without any questioning. My father warned me that my "Americanization" would lead me into trouble. I admitted to my rebelliousness, but I wanted to live in a home where respect and the right of communication were given to all members of the family. I wanted a democracy. Here of course, my problem was not unique to my culture, but one I shared with other children of immigrants.

Despite my experience with assimilation, I retained some values that I had learned from the Old Country. I still cherished my Catholic religion but I did not have the same close relationship with the church, for religious studies were prohibited in American public schools. I still gave my parents high respect, as expected by Filipino values, and I disciplined myself well concerning educational expectations.

After living in this country for ten years, I had experienced many luxuries not available in the Philippines. At first, things were difficult and life was not as perfect as I had previously expected, but it was definitely better than the situation we left behind. I remained proud of my ethnicity, but the American way of living gave me educational opportunities and a standard of living that would not have been possible in my native country. America, a melting pot of cultures, had permitted me to keep an open mind to new possibilities without being uprooted from older traditions.

Anh-Dao Nguyen (UC San Diego 1988)

Leaving Home

In writing this "Roots" essay, I felt very excited because I wanted very much to share my roots and ethnicity. But having no sources (other than my immediate family) or documents to research through, it was difficult for me to go back further than my paternal grandfather. I realized that my father is probably the most important influence in my life because he's given me a big part of my identity. He himself has experienced so many diverse cultures in his life that he's instilled a lot of roots in me and shaped a lot of my thinking. I'm very grateful to my father for sharing his past and a part of himself with me. This essay is very special to me because it is a personal revelation about my family's history through two generations.

My paternal grandfather passed away when I was only two years old. The only memories I had of him were of paying respects in front of his picture. At every visit to my grandmother, I was told to climb up a ladder to a loft-like attic where an altar of my grandfather was kept and bow down three times on my knees to pay my respects to him. Only after that could I come down and spend time with my paternal grandmother. The room was always spotless, and the altar always had a plate of fresh fruits and incense burning. I never got the chance to know my paternal grandfather, but hearing my parents talk about him makes me wish for a lifetime with him.

My grandfather Nguyen Duc De was born in 1900 in Lang-Can (fifty miles from Hanoi), province of Haiduong, the district of Thanh-Ha, North Vietnam. He joined the French army when he came of age and went to Marseilles, France, for five years. After returning home to Haiduong, he met and married my grandmother, Tang Thi Sung, in 1927. She was from the same province, and her family arranged for her to marry my grandfather. In 1927 their eldest son, Nguyen Duc De, was born. At this time, my grandfather cut hair for a living and my grandmother farmed the rice fields. In 1935 economic depression hit Haiduong, and my grandfather accepted a job in Shanghai, China, policing an area controlled by the French army.

During my grandfather's absence, my father had to assume the role of breadwinner. He first went begging but later hired out as a servant. This period in my father's life was crucial in shaping what he thinks and feels now. These years made him very bitter and cynical about the upper crust of society. He refers to the wealthy class by the word "capitalists." This word expresses best his feeling of resentment. My father said that the French, Americans, and Japanese taught the Vietnamese the evil of capitalism so he doesn't blame his countrymen for their corruption. He feels that a person cannot be rich and honest at the same time. In Vietnam there was so much corruption that the government couldn't even collect taxes. I feel that he sometimes draws on these years to push his children and make us realize that we can be rich and successful without forgetting who we are and where we come from.

From age twelve to sixteen, my father became a servant to any family that would hire him. He stayed for as long as they wanted and did anything that they told him to do. This included cooking and cleaning, working in the rice fields, feeding pigs, and even fetching water from a well at midnight. Growing up, I've heard many stories from my father's childhood that have often made me wonder how my father could have endured such years, much less have taken control of his life through hard work and turned it into a worthwhile living experience.

One of the stories that has stood out in my mind from all the rest describes my father as a houseboy for a woman who was the second cousin to his mother. This woman was very wealthy and ruthless. She worked my father from before dawn until late after dusk. And she never let him forget how lucky he was to have found work with her. She took every opportunity to humiliate him and was never on time in paying him. During one harvest, my father had to cook dinner for a work crew after helping in the fields all day himself. He fell asleep while watching the rice and burned the whole pot. The mistress whipped him mercilessly in front of everyone and made him clean pigpens all night instead of sleeping. She also withheld his wages for that week. The next morning, the mistress had company over and as my father served tea, the guest inquired who my father was. The mistress, being well-educated, replied in French that my father was nothing but a pitiful orphan beggar in the street that she took pity on and gave employment. Hearing this, my father (who understood French) packed what little belongings he had and left.

What made this story so significant in my mind was the fact that my father returned years later to help this woman, who became bedridden with illness with no one to care for her. He sent for a doctor and paid for her medical expenses and nursed her until she got well. She lived another ten years after that. My father never forgot how she had treated, or rather mistreated, a twelve-year-old boy; but he also never forgot that she was a distant relative who was sick and needed care. I am sure that God has never forgotten what he did either, because that one good deed has been repaid over and over again in my father's life and in his children's also.

After my father turned sixteen, he joined the Vietnamese revolutionaries called the Viet Minh. Their cause, opposing the French government, recruited many young men like my father who were very passionate against foreigners in Vietnam. He was captured by the French army one year later and imprisoned for three years. He was put in prison for being a spy during the war of the Viet Minh against the French. My father recalls, "I got caught by chance. A certain Lieutenant Obb, a Frenchman, caught me. He even shot at me while I was sitting in a chair. He'd been wounded by the Communists, so he was very angry. He thought I had a watch that the Viet Minh had taken from him."

My father left North Vietnam in February of 1948 because he had been a prisoner in a French camp. He had a feud going with an official's son and attacked the boy. The boy complained to his father so my father had to leave. He left the North by ship going to Singapore. He wanted to go to France but got sick on the ship and had to return to Vietnam and went to live in South Vietnam.

In Saigon, my father took odd jobs for three years. At twenty, he took a job for a French telecommunications company at the Saigon post office. After three years, he left to work for Air France, a French airline company. Three years later, he took a government job for the Vietnamese Federal Aviation Administration and became a civil servant until our departure in 1975.

"I never really thought about marriage," my father said, "but my father was a fortune-teller, so when I was twenty-seven he persuaded me that it was time to get married. So out of six girls, one was chosen and approved by him. I had not yet met her at this time but according to his fortune-telling books, the marriage would work out because our birth signs were compatible." This was in 1954 and that chosen girl was my mother, Le Thi Thao.

My father had already at this time gone back to Hanoi and picked up my paternal grandparents who were caught in the Communist area. The French let them come to Haiphong and he got them out of there in 1950. My father and his new bride lived together with his parents in one small house until the birth of my oldest brother, Nguyen Duc Trung, in 1955.

Fortunately, my grandparents were not very critical or demanding of their daughter-in-law, so my mother formed a very close and bonding relationship with her new parents-in-law. Along with my paternal grandmother, my mother wept painfully at the death of my grandfather in 1968 during the Tet Offensive.

In 1958, just a few months before my second brother was born, my parents moved to Tan Son Nhut because my father was offered government housing for being a civil servant. Tan Son Nhut was a large air base owned by the public works of Vietnam. It was divided into two parts—military and civilian. It was the only international airport in South Vietnam, so all commercial and military airplanes landed there.

By the time I was born in 1966, my parents already had five children and I was to be their last. I can honestly say that I have only happy memories of growing up in Tan Son Nhut. It was an ideal home. We were protected from outside civilians, and my playground was an air base where I often rode my bicycle and watched outside the gate as large machinelike birds would glide down and land gracefully. There was a military air base where American GIs were stationed. I became friends with many young soldiers who adopted me as their "pet." It was with them that I would practice the English that I had learned at home from my father. They often took me on their backs into the PX and bought me dolls and ordered pretty things from J. C. Penney catalogs.

My father never spoke much of his relatives in the North. All his uncles, aunts, and cousins (about fifty people) died in Hanoi in 1945 during the famine caused by the Japanese occupation, I later learned. My father said that the French, through bribes and connections, managed to escape the starvation. The French had divided the country into three areas, North, South, and Central, and had managed to set each area against the others. To this date, my father seems very deeply affected by the famine in North Vietnam. He talks vehemently about the pain of losing so many loved ones due to the despicably inhumane acts of the Japanese.

My father never had any formal education. He learned to write Vietnamese through private classes at night in Saigon. He also studied algebra and French (although he has spoken French most of his life, he never learned to read and write it until now). He never studied any other subjects except English. In 1956, when American advisers first came, he was a radio operator and studied English for five years since there were classes for civil servants. "I had no money for bribes, or friends in influential positions, so I was unable to come for a year to the U.S. as promised as a reward for the best student." My father also studied Morse code and teletype in Saigon in order to seek high-paying jobs with American firms at the time. For a man who has never had a basic education, my father managed to support his wife and six children, his mother and sisters, and also his wife's family.

In April 1975 a former American boss of my father, Mr. Allen, told him to contact twenty families for evacuation because they had just gotten word that American troops were withdrawing from Vietnam. My father was allowed to evacuate his family and himself with top priority to America. We were able to fly from our home (Tan Son Nhut) directly to Guam. We stayed there for one month, then we were taken to Camp Pendleton, and from there, straight to San Diego where we've resided ever since. We were sponsored by a Seventh-Day Adventist Church (because we had been Adventists in Vietnam), who helped us get started in our new life and even gave my father his first job here at the church.

The fateful night of our evacuation has left a large imprint in my mind. I remember my mother waking us all up in the middle of the night and telling us to pack one change of clothing each and be careful not to make any noise because our next-door neighbor was a military policeman for the South Vietnamese government. I wanted to take all my dolls with me, but my mother said no; she said we were only taking a short vacation and that we would return very soon. I felt very excited at the thought of going to America because I had heard so much about it from my American friends. Hours before, my mother had hidden many of our gold bars in the back of our house. She wanted to leave it for my oldest brother who was in the air force. He had no way of knowing that we would be evacuating because he was stationed at the time in the front line and we had not seen him for three months. It was a secret move that was not allowed to leak out. Whether or not my parents believed our evacuation was permanent or not, they kept telling us (perhaps to convince themselves) that our move was only temporary. I think doing this eased their consciences at the thought of leaving their oldest son behind.

That morning, as the bus drove us past our house heading for the airplane, my mother told the bus driver to stop the bus because she saw my oldest brother standing in front of our house. She insisted that my father bring my brother along with us. My father got off the bus to talk to my brother but after a while came back alone. He told us that my brother did not want to leave. He felt that he should stay and help his country fight the Communists. He also pointed out that he could take the gold bars that my mother hid and take care of my paternal grandmother and aunt who would be left behind with no one to care for them. My father made him promise that he would try and get out if things worsened in twenty-four hours. My brother promised, and this made my father feel better at leaving him behind. He never did make it out, though. At seventeen, my brother felt the same passionate feelings that my father felt when he joined the Vietnamese revolutionaries. My brother believed strongly in his country and was not about to abandon it in a time of trouble.

After we settled in San Diego our lives became routine. The children went to school and adapted very well. English has never been a barrier for us since my father taught us all to speak English at an early age. Pretty soon, we excelled in our studies and learned to grasp much of the American way of life. We were never allowed to speak English at home though. My parents knew how easy it was for children to forget their native tongue. This was one of the many preventive measures my parents took in keeping us from becoming uprooted.

We came to America because of the fall of Saigon. Our reasons for emigrating were political; it was simply a matter of life and death. If my father did not believe that our lives were endangered if we stayed, we would never have emigrated. Being poor again would not be anything new, and it would be the obvious consequence of immigration. With the fall of Saigon, the Vietcong would publicly execute anyone who had ever been associated with the Americans or the South Vietnamese government. If we had stayed, my father would have been one of the first in line to be executed. This fear made it possible for my father to leave his oldest son, his elderly mother, and his beloved country.

My father felt that the fall of Vietnam was caused by the U.S. government. He also felt that we lost Cambodia and Laos also because of the United States. "They caused the corruption of the system," he said. He also said that it would have been better if the United States had never interfered in Vietnam. All his life, my father has always found himself outside looking in, wanting what he sees and hating the privileged elite that apparently keep him out. Adjusting in America was not difficult for my father since his life patterns have accustomed him to absorb shock and have kept him from getting culturally stuck. My father said that he has a very mixed culture: Vietnamese, Chinese, French, Japanese, and now American. Obviously all these countries have played an important part in his life. He has been on his own since he was a small boy, has not enjoyed any privileged positions in his culture, and has repeatedly had to accommodate himself to new situations and places. My father feels that life is more ordered and formalized in the United States than in Vietnam. One has to make an appointment to see a doctor and even friends. We are controlled by social structure and must live within this instead of creating our own. In Vietnam, you never needed an appointment for anything.

Although my father is bitter about his past, he is optimistic about his future in the United States. He says that class differences are not so visible here. And here, his children all have a chance at a college education with hard work, not as in Vietnam where one needed money and influence.

We were always told that we had to do better than our classmates because of our skin color. Being yellow and Vietnamese is bad enough without lacking the knowledge and education that one needs to survive and succeed in a white society. Our father's cynicism and ambition is drilled into us and it has driven us to be more competitive and to give 200 percent at everything we have done. We were taught to always respect our culture and love our country no matter how far we have come. We are living proof that one can become successful without being uprooted. We have all become professionals in our fields, but we have never forgotten how we came here with only the clothes on our backs. We have become American citizens, and yet we have never given up our Vietnamese citizenship in our hearts. If we never get to return to our homeland, we will surely pass on our roots and culture to our children. Ours is not a struggle and triumph story that has ended here. Our triumph will be the day when we will be reunited with our relatives in our beloved homeland again. It will be the day when there will be peace again in Vietnam. In the meantime, we go on living and working hard to prove to other Americans that we are grateful for the opportunities that we are given—the opportunity to excel and succeed in a society where anyone can achieve success through hard work and dedication regardless of race and color. For this, we will always be grateful.

The Nguyen Children

Nguyen Duc Nam—b. 1/7/58—San Diego State University, B.S., Civil Engineering

Nguyen Viet Bac—b. 7/3/59—UC San Diego B.S., Mechanical Engineering; B.A., French Literature

Nguyen Anh-Tram—b. 10/23/60—UC San Diego B.A., Biochemistry
Nguyen Dung Viet—b. 7/7/63—UC Irvine, B.S., Electrical Engineering
Nguyen Anh-Dao—b. 8/29/66—UC San Diego Quantitative Economics and Decision Science/French Literature, Junior)

Postscript, 1994: After numerous failed attempts, we finally succeeded in bringing my oldest brother to the United States and were reunited with him in June 1992. Through many trips back to Vietnam and countless meetings and persuasion and finally bribes of Communist officials, my mother was able to move my brother to the top of the list of eligible departees. We are grateful for this reunion, but bitter at the seventeen years lost that can never be reclaimed in my brother's life. His imprisonment in the New Economic Zone and in concentration camps was due to our family's evacuation and my father's employment by American firms. Although we are still living in the United States, as long as we are together as a family we will work toward that final day of going home to a free and peaceful Vietnam.

Lila Shah (SUNY Binghamton 1990)

Being Indian in America: My Ethnic Roots and Me

My heritage and ethnic roots are the foundation of my self. I am fortunate enough to know my roots and appreciate them. My life changed dramatically thirteen years ago when my family and I emigrated from India. The immigration experience transformed my life and me, personally. I have had the advantage of enjoying both cultures and understanding how they have shaped my life.

My family was a part of the Indian middle class. Unlike America, middle class in India meant a life of daily struggle and marginal economic mobility. Typically, the rich got richer, the poor got poorer, and the middle class got nowhere. This situation and pollution problems, which aggravated my father's health, compelled us to leave India. My aunt (father's sister) sponsored us in 1976, and my parents decided that my father would precede us to America where he would look for job opportunities and a place to live. While my father was gone, my mother would begin to pack up our apartment.

On a rainy evening when the smell of rain hung so heavy in the air that I still remember it today, my parents told us of their plans. My father stressed the lack of opportunities for my sister and me in India and the wealth of opportunity in America. Naturally, my sister and I were completely against the move and we were very vocal. My sister was ten and I was six, and India was all we had ever known. Opportunities, education, and careers were remote ideas.

My father left, and for the next year, I prayed that he would not find a

Shah family photo, Dhoraji, India, 1970; the family had gathered for the funeral of Lila Shah's paternal grandfather. Lila's father is second from the right; her mother is at the extreme left.

Lila Shah riding a horse on Juhu Beach, Bombay, 1973.

job or housing. I had no desire to move to a country ten thousand miles away for concepts I could barely understand. However, my father did find a job and a nice apartment in Syracuse, New York. So in 1977, I left with my mother and sister. At the airport, all our relatives and friends came to say goodbye. The departure was one of the most traumatic experiences of my life. I felt I was leaving behind everything I knew and venturing into an unknown chapter of my life. The resentment I felt against my parents that night was almost tangible.

Upon arriving in America, we were reunited with my father, and he attempted to explain all the good he had discovered in this country. Our apartment was the first thing I marveled at. In Bombay there had been an acute water shortage for as long as I could remember. This resulted in twenty minutes of water a day for all those living in Bombay. Even now, this seems tremendously difficult for me to comprehend. In our new apartment I quickly discovered that running water was available twenty-four hours a day. Many times I awoke in the middle of the night and watched the water run out of the faucet.

Besides these small amenities, it took time to adjust to life in America. School was a new experience as I quickly realized that I was the only Indian in the second grade and in my whole school. Luckily my school in India was conducted in English, so I was completely fluent. Aside from speaking English with a British accent, I was very much like other second graders.

My elementary school is the institution I credit with my assimilation. It was there that I learned about relationships and American customs. For example, a foreigner in my school in India would have been respected, and everyone in the class would have tried to become friends with that person. In the United States, instead, I was looked on as something of an oddity due to my darker skin color and different name. Although people were not outwardly cruel to me, they were not friendly either. I was treated with polite indifference. Relationships between boys and girls were also much more forward than in India. The way school was conducted in America was also different. In India, I had to stand up to answer questions, and there was always the chance of being hit by the teacher at any time. After coming to America, I really believed that students did not respect their teachers since they did not stand to answer questions. At school, I began to learn American customs and jargon as quickly as I could. The different qualities I possessed were not appreciated in a country where uniformity was stressed.

Uniformity manifested itself in many ways in American life. Reciting the pledge required everyone to stand in similar fashion and place their right hands over their hearts. My fellow students dressed basically the same, and

Lila Shah (right) with her older sister, Surya, Liverpool, New York, 1978.

there was always a rush to buy what everyone else was buying. Those who looked or acted different, like me, were regarded with scorn. As soon as I realized this, I attempted to change all the things about me that made me different. For a period of five to six years, I completely denied my cultural and ethnic roots. At home I was an Indian girl who spoke an Indian language and ate Indian food. When my parents socialized with their friends (all of whom were Indian), I was Indian. But at school, the shopping mall, in restaurants, I was as American as I could be. I dressed in American clothes and would flatly refuse if my mother of father asked me to go somewhere dressed in my Indian clothes. I spoke slang and tried very hard to be viewed as an American. I would speak only English when I was out of my home and insisted my parents do the same. Suddenly, I was fourteen years old and I felt like two different people.

The following year was very difficult for me as I tried to be one person or the other depending on the situation. I spent many months thinking and finally came to the conclusion that I had to resolve this duality. I was no longer capable of being two people; somewhere inside of me was the real me. I spent the better part of that year rediscovering my ethnic roots. I realized that I was Indian and the blood of a ten-thousand-year culture ran deep in my veins. I began to participate frequently in Indian activities. I participated in the Festival of Nations, a Syracuse program that allowed different countries to set up booths for a weekend selling their native food and clothing. At the end of each evening, each country would perform an ethnic dance before an audience of hundreds of people. I was filled with pride that by participating in the dance, I was enabling others to enjoy my culture. I came to the startling conclusion that instead of hiding my Indian roots, I could share them with others. I was surprised at the number of people who were interested in my culture and wanted to know more about it. Rather than hiding my differences, I could reveal them. It was nice to be a little different from other people.

In spite of finding my Indian roots, I also realized that the impact of America on me could not be denied. It would have been completely incorrect of me to believe that I had not taken anything from this culture. America had also contributed to my development. Some of my values I realized were American, and I had adopted some aspects of popular culture. My taste in music, clothes, and television was quite American. On the other hand, my religion, food, and most of my morals remained Indian. Instead of regretting the fact that I was a part of two cultures, I began to enjoy it. I was a much richer and more balanced person because I knew of two different cultures. I had the advantage of picking and choosing aspects of both cultures that I wanted to retain or discard. Many people would never have the opportunity to make such choices. I realized I was a more interesting and well-traveled person because I had experienced things many of my peers never would.

My parents' situation is a bit different. My parents are staunchly Indian in their beliefs and in the way they lead their lives. My family is decidedly patriarchal, and though my father is not domineering, he does have the power in the family. We eat only Indian food in the house and speak, largely, our native tongue. All my parents' friends are Indian and neither of my parents feels deprived because of this. They find the morals of this country generally lacking and believe that American popular culture is the only culture of this nation. Perhaps this may sound as if my parents do not like Americans, but this is not true. They like my friends and my father's coworkers. They simply do not agree with some of the aspects of American culture like drinking, dating, divorce, and the style of American individualism that stresses the "me" over anyone else—including parents.

My father has a deep abiding respect for America, resulting from the fact that he came to this country with only thirteen dollars and has since achieved success on a large scale (monetarily, socially, etc.). Of course now my father believes that anyone, no matter what their circumstances, can achieve the American dream. My mother also believes these things and the idea that women are equal to men.

In the past, friction has occurred between me and my parents as I attempted to assert my American characteristics that were directly opposed to their Indian beliefs. On the whole, however, my parents have assimilated very well to this country and culture. Rather than being too liberal or too conservative, they have handled each situation individually with a mixture of Indian and American tools. I consider myself very fortunate when I see some of my other Indian friends who have very strict and conservative parents that do not realize that this country is not India.

Today, I am part Indian and part American and not sorry about it at all. I enjoy all the opportunities and avenues of mobility provided by this nation. I am an aspiring lawyer and frequently compare who I am here to who I could have been had I remained in India. I have realized that I could never live in India again, but this fact does not upset me. I feel as if I belong, and I believe I have carved out a niche for myself in this country. I feel tremendous gratitude toward my parents when I think about all the upheaval they went through for their children. My ethnic roots are something I want to give to my children so they too can see how their heritage can weave itself into the fabric of their lives and enrich it.

Vladimir Sinayuk (SUNY Binghamton 1990)

My Immigrant Experience

On May 11, 1976 my parents and I landed at Kennedy Airport in New York. We were newly arrived immigrants from the Soviet Union, originating from a town called Chernovtzi, in the Southwestern Ukraine Republic. Fourteen years later, the Sinayuk family is a typical middle-class Long Island household. All those years ago, however, the novelty of the American land and Western freedom had not yet overshadowed the misery that we, and many like us, had risen out of.

As Jewish citizens of the Soviet Union, our premigration lives and motivations for migrating were common to many. In 1975 Chernovtzi had a Jewish population of one hundred thousand, about one-third of the total. However, the existence of a practicing Jewish community was suppressed to the point of invisibility. Chernovtzi had been Rumanian till just prior to the outbreak of World War II. The city became a haven for Holocaust survivors after the war, including my maternal grandparents. Stalin inherited a thriving Jewish community, by then a rarity in the Soviet Union. He proceeded to close all but one tiny synagogue. (One Catholic and one Russian Orthodox church were also left standing as "showpieces" to Western visitors.) When my mother and father went to school, they were taught Communist principles of the nonsense and evil of religion. The school administration practiced public humiliation when there was evidence that a child was religiously active, to encourage him or her to stop and to deter others.

Besides the lack of religious freedom, being Jewish in Chernovtzi meant having one's opportunities limited even further than that of the average person. My mother was a brilliant student in high school, graduating second in her class. However, she had to go all the way to Siberia to study engineering because it was impossible for a Jewish candidate, even such a successful one, to be accepted to an institution in the especially anti-Semitic Ukraine. At the Tomsk Polytechnic Institute (in Siberia), nobody knew that she was Jewish. With her departure, my mother's mother, who had been recently widowed, was left on her own to support herself and her two young daughters. My mother describes the social security system, supposedly the forte of Communist nations, as miserable. My grandmother received barely any support from the government as she struggled just to survive. Meanwhile, my father was serving out his required stint in the army, which at the time was three years.

Looking back on life in Chernovtzi from the standpoint of fourteen prosperous years in America, my mother estimates the standard of living there to be ten times lower. The popular notions of public lines for food (and toilet paper) are not false. My mother recalls frequently being the one whose turn had come up just as the supplies ran out, wasting hours in line. Of course, there was no private property. All housing had to be applied for and granted, and a newly-wed Jewish couple had low priority. The apartment in which I first lived was a tiny room, with a bathroom shared with three other apartments. We were lucky enough to receive my grandmother's apartment, with a private bathroom, once she and my mother's younger sisters left for Israel late in 1973.

The inevitability of immigration gradually became apparent to my parents. Their financial situation was a major consideration. My mother was earning a miserable salary, especially for someone with a master's degree in chemical engineering, and had to pay half of it every month for that apartment with the bathroom we shared with three other families. Including his army service, my father had been working full time since he was sixteen (my mother and he met at the night high school). He went on to night college for mechanical engineering after the army, while he worked during the day. The three of us got by decently for the average young Jewish family, but the future was not very promising. Not only were job advancement possibilities limited for my parents because of their ethnicity, but even with the promotions they managed to receive, salary raises were meager. A comfortable life with financial security did not seem in store for us.

The most important reason to emigrate, however, was the allure of freedom. My parents were disturbed about the Soviet education system, and it had not changed by the time I entered it. The teachers tried to brainwash Communist ideals into the children's heads from an early age, even though only a tiny minority of Soviet citizens were members of the Communist party. Religious training was nonexistent, so my parents grew up almost completely ignorant of their own religious traditions. The status of Jews in the Soviet Union had not changed very much since the days of the Pale of Settlement. Though Chernovtzi was a largely Jewish town, it was situated in the intensely anti-Semitic Ukrainian Republic. My parents had a very clear understanding of all this during their formative years and their early lives together. My mother said the breaking point, the incident that pushed my family into initiating the immigration process, occurred one day when I returned from nursery school. I recited to her a poem about "Grandpa" Lenin. She decided then and there that she had had enough of Soviet society, that I deserved a better future, and that we were leaving Chernovtzi and the Soviet Union.

My parents applied for immigration visas, and three months later, we received them. In the meantime, though, my parents were harassed by their superiors at work for wanting to join the enemy in the United States. They received demotions, and were threatened with job termination. We lost our apartment a month prior to our departure and were forced to live with my father's parents (who joined us in the United States a year after our arrival). Even with the humiliation and harassment my family received, my mother said that friends and coworkers said they were envious of us because we were headed for freedom and normal lives. As enemies of the state, we flew from Moscow Airport in January 1976. We were virtually penniless; the government had taken all our rubles to pay for the departing flight and the "cost" of the foreign passports.

The transition to Western culture was made smoother because of our four-month stay in Italy, which at the time was the midway point for Russian immigrants. As they waited for American visas, my parents were shocked by the variety and excess they saw in the supermarkets. There was nothing that even remotely resembled a supermarket in Chernovtzi. The relative prosperity of Italy prepared us well for the opulence on display in the United States. My mother said she could not understand the causes when she witnessed Communist demonstrations in Italy. There seemed no logic in them, especially when viewed from our background.

Our passage from Italy to America, and our stay in Italy, was paid for by the New York–based H.I.A.S. (Hebrew Immigrant Aid Society). They also provided English teachers for my parents in both Italy and New York. When we first arrived in America, we stayed for a short time with friends in the Bronx. Immediately, we began to be supported by N.Y.A.N.A.

(New York Association for New Americans). They provided a social worker who arranged for Medicaid, since my mother was pregnant with my sister. N.Y.A.N.A. supported us for our first year in America, paying for our Bronx apartment, while helping my parents acquire green cards, prepare résumés, and in turn find secure jobs. By the end of 1976, the Sinayuk family was well on its way to a happy American life; my sister was born and I was attending Yeshiva for kindergarten, while my parents were employed at their professions.

My parents describe their assimilation into American life as a purely positive experience. Never was there any nostalgia for Soviet life, even when my parents took four trains each way, between work on Long Island and home in the Bronx. Life here at its worst was vastly superior to life there at its best. The most important factor in the ease of the adjustment was the ready access to training in the English language. Even when English was still new to them, my parents were able to communicate with their neighbors in the Bronx through Yiddish.

I was only five years old when I entered school in America. Therefore, my education in the English language was easy and shortly complete, perhaps as much through television as through school. I was much too young to experience, appreciate, or retain my earlier experiences once in the United States. Sometimes, I think I am no different than if I were born in this country. Yet, I feel ethnicity has had a profound impact on my life. My background has made me extremely appreciative of Jewish culture. I realize that I might not have ever expressed my Judaism had I remained where I was born. I would not have been able to visit Jerusalem and the Western Wall for my Bar Mitzvah, nor indeed to have a Bar Mitzvah at all, as my father was deprived. Being an immigrant, instead of a native American, makes me appreciate that much more not only my ethnic background, but especially the freedom and opportunity the United States offers.

Puwat Charukamnoetkanok (SUNY Binghamton 1990)

Triple Identity: My Experience as an Immigrant in America

"America is the land of opportunity." Is this a myth or reality? I came to America four years ago with a faith that I would find opportunity here. However, I realize a reality: racism exists and most people will not easily accept immigrants. In the spring of 1990, I took a course, "Immigration and Ethnicity in the United States," in which I learned that I am not alone. Many immigrants encountered similar barriers. My grandparents are also immigrants, and I have learned about their experiences. In this essay, I compare the experiences of my paternal grandparents with my own experiences.

In 1937 my grandfather, whom I call Ar-kong, came to Thailand from Ch'eng-Hai in Teochiu state (in southern China). He was thirteen years old. His mother brought him to meet his father, who was attracted by the economic opportunity of Thailand and had left China to open a jewelry store in Nakornrajsima (my birthplace, northeast of Bangkok). Great-grandfather had a second wife who was Thai, which was not an uncommon phenomenon for there were many benefits. Because he was far from home, she was his companion. The marriage also served economic purposes; she could speak Thai, which was good for business. However, the two wives were like oil and water, which put the family under pressure. For this reason, Ar-kong developed a keen sense of self-reliance and independence. He married my grandmother, Ar-ma, the daughter of a rice mill owner. The bridegroom and the bride were eighteen and seventeen years old, respectively. When Ar-kong was twenty-five years old, he opened his own jewelry store, which has been in business ever since.

Puwat Charukamnoetkanok's grandparents, Ar-Kong and Ar-Ma, in China, ca 1993.

Chinese and Thai are technically the same race. Thai people are believed to have migrated from the southern part of China hundreds of years ago. However, Thailand and its cultures were also influenced by India and ancient Cambodia, thereby distinguishing Chinese and Thai both physically and culturally. This resulted in ethnic prejudice. "The Thai consider the Chinese uncouth because they are often loud and raucous in public, because they are noisy eaters, and have other food habits which the Thai deem very undesirable."[1] This uneasiness would not have led to extensive prejudice had it not been exacerbated by the Thais' apprehension of economic competition from the Chinese. The majority of Thai people are engaged in agriculture, and they blame Chinese middlemen for low crop prices and high prices in stores. However, this rationalization is belied by the fact that there are many merchants who are not Chinese, and fluctuations of prices depend on many other factors, not just the Chinese merchants.

Anti-Chinese sentiment reached its pinnacle during World War II, when all aliens (the majority were Chinese) were forced to evacuate the big cities and relocate to the countryside. Soon after their marriage, my grandparents had to move to Bou Yai (a small town near Nakornrajsima). It is interesting to note the similarity of this development and the evacuation of the Japanese from the West Coast of the United States during the same period. National security was the official reason in both cases, but I believe that the desire to undermine the economic prosperity of the evacuees was the real intention. However, the two practices were by no means equivalent; the Chinese in Thailand suffered much less from this experience. They were not subjected to incarceration and could move their businesses with them. Ar-kong helped his father run a new store in Bou Yai, but the business was not as good because there were fewer customers. The evacuation lasted for four years, and during this period my father was born. Then the family moved back to Nakornrajsima.

My grandparents ignored the prejudice they faced. They worked hard, hoping that when they became established economically people would accept them for who they really were—kind, generous, and peaceful persons. I believe they have succeeded.

Ar-kong and Ar-ma also tried their best to assimilate. They sent my father and his brothers and sister to Thai schools, and the children only learned Chinese in the evening. Ar-kong and Ar-ma learned to speak Thai. Ar-ma worked especially hard in her endeavor to learn Thai. Night after night, she would learn how to read, write, and speak Thai from Thai literature. I, a naughty grandson, used to make fun of her awkward, "out-of-the-book" vocabulary. My grandparents and parents would not let me forget about Chinese holidays, but they also observed Thai holidays, which was fine with me for I had more days off from school. Like most Chinese immigrants to Thailand, my grandparents showed their respect and gratitude toward the Thai royal family and taught their children and grandchildren to do the same.

The ultimate act of assimilation came when Ar-kong and Ar-ma changed their nationality to Thai. They changed their last name from Wong which means yellow in Chinese to Charukamnoetkanok, Thai words for the city where gold comes from. There is a funny story that accompanies this change of surname. When Ar-kong registered to change his last name, he submitted three different choices. But all three had already been used, so a kind officer scrambled them together and came up with this wonderful but long last name. I am not quite sure if I should thank or blame that officer for making my name easily recognized but too long to fit in any provided space.

Because of my grandparents' willingness to assimilate and the generous attitude of the majority of Thai people, I never experienced an identity crisis in Thailand. To me, having Chinese ancestry was another fact, just like being a male. It was not something to think about. I was born in Thailand, therefore I was Thai. The fact that Chinese and Thai are physically different was never obvious to me—or at least not until I came to America.

In April 1986 I was told that we would go to America. I only knew about America from movies and television shows, and was very eager to see tall buildings and advanced technology. I said goodbye to all my friends, all of whom were envious of me. My uncle brought us—my brothers, my sister, and myself—to meet our parents who had left earlier to look for a house, school, and business. We traveled by Korea Airlines. The plane stopped at Taiwan, Korea, Japan, Hawaii, and finally New York. We rented a house in Elmont for a few months until the closing of the purchase of our house in Valley Stream. When we went to New York City, I saw tall buildings just like in the movies. But I experienced many things that have never been shown accurately by Hollywood.

The major difference between my immigration and my grandparents' is the motivation. Ar-kong migrated from China mainly for economic reasons. My parents' main objective for migrating was the education of their children. This point can be proven by the fact that my parents left their established business behind and have started from scratch in America. Circumstances in China and Thailand prevented my grandfather Ar-kong from providing his son an education. My father left high school to work, and that kept him from reaching his full potential. He had no choice but to follow his father in the jewelry business.

Puwat Charukamnoetkanok (extreme right) and his siblings in Hawaii, 1986; this was the family's first stop in the United States.

However, both migration experiences are similar in many ways. For the first time in my life, I have learned about prejudice and discrimination. I have been taught to be nice to others, which includes people who are "different" from myself. But I have learned, in America, that not everybody has been taught that way. Many people judge a person only on appearances. I have not yet experienced prejudice directly. Nobody has ever called me by derogatory terms or beaten me because of the color of my skin. But knowing of the existence of racism has affected me just the same. I will not blame the racists, but I cannot keep from feeling sorry for them, for they have lost the opportunity to meet potential friends because they are narrow-minded.

Like my grandparents, I also experience difficulty regarding language. Now I feel very bad for making fun of Ar-ma. I have realized how hard it is to learn another language. An inability to communicate is very frustrating. I become hypersensitive sometimes because I am constantly not sure what people are saying around me. Speaking with a strange accent makes me become self-conscious. There are many times when I feel that it is difficult to articulate my thoughts.

In America, there are many cultural differences that I have to learn. For example there are many occasions where I feel totally lost, as when my friends talk about TV shows before 1986. Many values are different. I, like many children from Asia, have been taught to respect elders, including parents, relatives, and teachers. Needless to say, it is quite different here in America. I do not understand why, since you lose nothing by giving respect. This essay would not have been possible without these marvelous people. I also meet Chinese friends who have never been in Thailand; people who look just like me but are not Thai.

Living in America, I learn about racism and cultural differences, and experience language difficulties. For the first time, I experience an identity crisis. While most immigrants have double identities to deal with, I have three. Am I Chinese, Thai, or American? At times, I am very confused and angry. No matter which identity I choose, I will be different. However, I will never be able to solve this crisis if I care too much about what other people think. I cannot change their thoughts, but I can change mine. Ar-kong and Ar-ma ignored people who were prejudiced against them in Thailand, and I should be able to do the same in America. I do not really have to choose.

I have a unique opportunity to combine the good qualities of each identity into one. This is, of course, easier said than done. But at least now that I know what to do, achieving the goal can be done with less distraction.

If I am willing to work hard at it, hopefully some day people will accept me for who I am. America is really a land of opportunity, but as with all good land, hard work and patience are needed to harvest the crops.

Note

1. Richard J. Coughlin, *Double Identity: The Chinese in Modern Thailand* (Hong Kong: Hong Kong University Press, 1960), 81.

Rose Rameau (SUNY Binghamton 1994)

Two Poems Translated by Carrol Coates

RÉFLEXION

Haïti! Haïti!
Haïti, rose noire.
Ne vois-tu pas qu'ils ont trahi?
Belle négresse,
Ils ont arraché tes dernières feuilles vertes . . . .
De toi ils se sont moqués,
Ils t'ont accusée . . . de tout. . . .
Femme vaillante,
Ils ont même oublié
Que tu es la perle des Antilles.
Haïti, fleur printanière,
Conserveras-tu ton nom. . . ?
Pourquoi t'es-tu endormie?
Réveille-toi!
Va sauver tes enfants qui meurent de faim!
Leurs parents sont maltraités,
Isolés, exilés, éparpillés partout.
Haïti, pays noir
Premier à prendre ta liberté.
Oh, que j'attends de toi quelques feuilles.
Oui, quelques feuilles vertes de ton jardin.

REFLECTION

Haiti! Haiti!
Haiti, black rose.
Don't you see that they have betrayed you?
Beautiful black woman,
They wrenched away your last green leaves. . . .
They mocked you,
Accused you . . . of everything. . . .
Courageous woman,
They even forgot
That you are the Pearl of the Antilles.
Haiti, spring flower,
Can you keep your name. . . ?
Why did you fall asleep?
Wake up!
Run to save your starving children!
Their parents are mistreated,
Isolated, exiled, scattered across the globe.
Haiti, black country,
the first to seize your freedom!
Oh, how I long for your green leaves.
Yes, a few green leaves from your garden.

BAJO ESTE CIELO

Bajo este cielo que no parece duro,
Donde reina la angustia, el dolor. . . el castigo
Todavía nadie ha encontrado una cura.
El sueño de Martin Luther King.
La lucha de Malcom X,
¿A dónde llegaremos?

¡Ay! . . me siento triste de ver
y oír gritos de mis hermanos
  Por la libertad. . .
Sí, la libertad de ser negro,
La libertad de vivir como humano
  Ese orgullo que vive
al fondo de nuestro corazón,
Nos empuja a dispararnos.

Lucrecia, una de las víctimas,
Tan joven, tan inocente para entrar en los cielos.
Hermana caribeña, hermana de corazón.
Ojalá que tu Dios te ayude.

¡Ay! Lucrecia, hermana de mi tierra. . .
si hay un Dios en los cielos,
El infierno está sobre la tierra.
¿Pagarán ellos por sus pecados?

BENEATH THIS SKY

Beneath this sky, which does not look hard,
Where anxiety, pain and punishment hold sway.
Nobody has yet found a cure.
The dream of Martin Luther King.
The struggle of Malcolm X,
Where are we going?

Ay! I feel sad when I see
And hear the shouts of my brothers
    Claiming freedom . . .
Yes, the freedom to be black,
The freedom to live as humans,
    that pride dwelling
In the depths of our heart
Makes us explode.

Lucrecia, one of the victims,
So young and innocent to be sent to heaven.
Caribbean sister, sister of my heart.
May God succor you.

Ay! Lucrecia, sister from my land,
If there is a God in heaven,
Hell is above the earth.
Will they pay for their sins?

Afterword

What are we to make of these accounts—of the thirty essays and two poems that students at the University of California, San Diego, and the State University of New York at Binghamton wrote in an immigration history course between 1977 and 1994? A skeptical reader might find them interesting yet pose the question, Are they true?

I would respond by quoting from Studs Terkel, in his introduction to the collection *Hard Times: An Oral History of the Great Depression:* "This is a memory book, rather than one of hard fact and precise statistic." Addressing the truthfulness of his respondents, Terkel quoted an exchange among Pa and Tom Joad and Preacher Casy in John Steinbeck's *Grapes of Wrath:*

> Pa said, "S'pose he's tellin' the truth—that fella?" The preacher answered, "He's tellin' the truth, awright. The truth for him. He wasn't makin' nothin' up." "How about us?" Tom demanded. "Is that the truth for us?" "I don' know," said Casy.

Terkel reflected on the relevance of this fictional passage to the interviews he'd conducted: "I suspect the preacher spoke for the people in this book, too. In their rememberings are their truths." So I would judge for the students writing about their ethnic roots in this collection.[1]

One thing is clear from these essays—students used the occasion to construct the current meaning of ethnicity in their lives. One's ethnicity is the product of historical experience working upon an evolving sense of oneself. It is not a biological given; it is not even the simple result of being a member of a particular social group. In these papers students bring together their own experiences and conversations they have had with their parents and other relatives, and construct a "script" that explains to themselves and to readers how they have come to view their ethnicity in the way they have. They view the experiences of grandparents and parents in a teleological way, as events that shaped the kind of people they (the authors) have become and the attitudes toward ethnicity they hold as they write their papers.[2] We see the "ethnicity" of each student at a particular point in its evolution—at another time, each student would undoubtedly offer a somewhat different picture.

In reading these essays I have been struck by the revelations they provide of changing cultural patterns in the United States. If one had access to similar immigrant family stories written eighty years ago, one might find many more references to trade unions. Given that the forebears of these student authors often worked as laborers, in coal mines, and in garment shops, the references to trade union activities are surprisingly scanty. The authors recall relatives buying land or starting their own businesses far more frequently than they mention labor or political radicalism. Tanya Mlodzinski's grandfather and father were active in Finnish-American radical circles, but they stand alone. The relative invisibility of trade union activity or political radicalism in these accounts no doubt reflects the decline of the labor movement and of leftist politics in the post–World War II years. Such movements have not been important in these students' lives; consequently they play little part in the family stories they reconstruct.

While class issues are muted in these accounts, instances of racial and ethnic conflict are more readily acknowledged. Such incidents are more common in the stories of recent immigrants than in the recollections of grandparents, reflecting in part the greater immediacy of recent events, but also the changing racial and ethnic composition of immigrants. Stories of European immigrants—as in the Carnicelli, Koch, and Turetzky accounts—are more likely to detail discrimination in the Old Country than in the United States. Hispanic writers, in contrast, frequently comment on the pervasiveness of racial discrimination in the United States. Thus Josephine Burgos found herself placed in classes with non-English speakers simply because of her Latin American last name. Shana Rivas's father, who felt that the color barrier made it impossible for him to assimilate into American society, returned to Puerto Rico. And Lizette Aguilar's dark-skinned Peruvian father so internalized this country's color consciousness that he married a white Puerto Rican and became upset when his teenage daughter dated a black person.

Racial taunts and epithets appear frequently in the stories of Asian Americans. Philippine-born Cecilia Pineda was called "Chink" and "Jap" by Maryland high school classmates. Both of Sang-Hoon Kim's parents faced racial harassment, and even though he was born in Flushing, New York, his ninth-grade classmates picked fights with him and hurled racial taunts. He felt "completely rejected" by those outside his family circle. Asian American students write about their steady assimilation into American culture, but conflict and ostracism are integral elements in this larger process. Many of the accounts remind us of how central race consciousness is in interpersonal relations in the United States today.

These essays speak to important elements of American culture; they also reflect changing scholarly views of immigration. Key points in the analysis offered by Virginia Yans McLaughlin (quoted in the introduction) are confirmed repeatedly in the students' accounts of their families' immigration and ethnic experiences.

First, the American immigration of these families is only part of a larger, worldwide migration phenomenon. For a fair number of these families, immigration was not a single, abrupt move, but a series of migrations. For Tanya Mlodzinski's forebears the path ran from Finland to Canada or the Great Lakes region and then to Yonkers, New York. Puwat Charukamnoetkanok's family migrated in two stages, first from China to Thailand and then to the United States. Ann Fenech's grandfather migrated from Malta to the United States and then to Tunisia. Years later his son emigrated once again, settling permanently in the United States. Three generations in Catherine Tagudin's family emigrated from the Philippines to the United States, beginning in the 1920s, but only when Catherine and her mother came in the 1970s did the migration become permanent. For the Mexican Americans and Puerto Ricans among these student authors, migration back and forth across borders was also a common phenomenon.

Second, the cultural transformations described in these essays are not all linear examples of straightforward assimilation into "American" ways. For some families—the Kitkos, Kochs, Turetzkys, and Pinedas are probably the best examples—assimilation is the dominant pattern across generations. For others, however, cultural developments are more uneven. For Virginia Correia's forebears, repeated marriages to new immigrants from Terceira kept alive Azorean traditions. Among immigrants of color and African Americans, continuing patterns of discrimination and strong group allegiances have kept ethnic identification strong even with the passage of time. Thus LaToya Powell is less concerned with integrating into the wider white culture than was her North Carolina–born grandfather.

So, too, Jaime Dominguez overcame his need to imitate his Anglo classmates in dress and speech. He learned he could be a Mexicano and still strive to succeed in American society. Lizette Aguilar articulates most clearly the alternative perspective that is evident in a fair number of these accounts: "For me the word assimilation has a negative meaning. For me it means to sell out into a culture that is not your own and so to deny your true family heritage. I am very proud that my parents did not assimilate into American culture because then I wouldn't be the person I am today."

Assimilation initially was viewed as a process through which immigrants came to accept the dominant Anglo-American culture as their own. Thus, in the early twentieth century immigrants were ranked by native-born Americans along a hierarchy in terms of their perceived assimilability. The national quotas set under the 1924 Johnson-Reid Act reflected these dominant perceptions, permitting admission to northern and western Europeans over those from southern and eastern Europe, and totally excluding Asian immigrants.

The essays in this collection help us to see the inadequacy of that formulation. Assimilation is not simply an either-or phenomenon, and the "American" culture to which immigrants accommodate is not static. One's allegiance to the culture of one's homeland may become diluted, not because one becomes "Americanized," but because of intermarriage. Thus Karen Gryga's Tyrolean mother married a Polish American and their children identified with both sets of inherited cultural traditions. Similarly, Susan Carnicelli acknowledges her Austrian and Italian, Jewish and Catholic roots. Melissa Algranati's complex cultural roots defy classification. As the daughter of an Egyptian Sephardic Jewish father and a Puerto Rican Catholic mother, she takes pride in being an "other" when forced to record her ethnicity on standardized forms. Bob Vaage provides the ultimate example of the ethnic blending evident among the authors in this collection, noting Irish and Norwegian ancestors on his father's side and Kwahadi Comanches on his mother's.

The ethnic diversity of the San Diego and Binghamton students represented in this volume reminds us of the hybrid nature of the "American" today. Their stories make clear that what it means to be an American is ever evolving, a fact brought home most strikingly by the prediction in *Time* magazine that by the year 2056 "white Americans will become a minority group."[3] The French-born Crèvecoeur's comments on the immigrant origins of the "new" American in the 1780s remain true today. Karen Gryga makes much the same point in her essay, quoting a Tyrolean immigrant who speaks eloquently in his recently acquired English: "Only the Indian is American citizen, that isn't a foreigner. Otherwise I don't care what nationality you are, you[r] father, or your grandfather, I don't care who it was, they all come from over across."[4] Would that all Americans—especially those more comfortably situated and more powerful—could appreciate his insight.

Notes

1. Studs Terkel, *Hard Times: An Oral History of the Great Depression* (1970; reprint, New York: Avon, 1971), 17.

2. For thoughtful discussions of how memories shift over time as one's relations to past events change, see Robert E. McGlone, "Rescripting a Troubled Past: John Brown's Family and the Harpers Ferry Conspiracy," *Journal of American History* 75 (March 1989): 1179–1200, and John Bodnar, "Power and Memory in Oral History: Workers and Managers at Studebaker," *Journal of American History* 75 (March 1989): 1201–21.

3. *Time,* 9 April 1990, p. 28, as quoted in Ronald Takaki, *A Different Mirror* (Boston: Little, Brown, 1993), 2.

4. Rita Cominolli, *Smokestacks Allegro: The Story of Solvay, a Remarkable Industrial/Immigrant Village (1880–1920)* (New York: Center for Migration Studies, 1990), 77.

Sample Roots Paper Topic

State University of New York at Binghamton
Department of History
History 264, Spring 1990

Write a six- to eight-page, typed, double-spaced paper discussing your own ethnic roots. Trace your maternal and paternal forebears. If immigrant, where did they come from? What can you learn about their lives before migration, their motivations in coming, and their initial experiences in this country? Move beyond description and discuss what you can learn about your ancestors' changing relations to American society. What evidence is there of your forebears' acceptance or rejection of assimilation? If it seems appropriate, discuss the influence ethnicity has had on your life.

Notes on Contributors

Lizette Aguilar grew up in the northern part of the Bronx and attended the High School of the Performing Arts. She is currently a student at the State University of New York at Binghamton with a double major in Literature and Rhetoric, and Latin American and Caribbean Studies. She hopes to teach and do college counseling with high school students.

Melissa Algranati graduated from Stuyvesant High School in New York City and is a student at the State University of New York at Binghamton. She is majoring in History and Philosophy, Politics, and Law. She has worked for three years at the Henry Street Settlement on the Lower East Side. She hopes some day to change the world, one argument at a time.

Peter Bosco grew up in the Bensonhurst neighborhood of Brooklyn and graduated from the State University of New York at Binghamton in 1992 with a major in Biology. He is currently a student at Tufts University School of Medicine.

Josephine Burgos is a 1994 graduate of the State University of New York at Binghamton with a major in English. She is currently doing graduate study at Syracuse University in English Education and hopes to teach at the high school or university level.

Susan Carnicelli graduated from the State University of New York at Binghamton in 1993 with a major in Geology. She is currently employed by an environmental consulting firm as a hydrogeologist.

Puwat Charukamnoetkanok immigrated to the United States from Thailand in 1986 and graduated from the State University of New York at Binghamton in 1992 with a major in Biochemistry. He is currently enrolled at the University of Rochester School of Medicine.

Virginia Correia graduated from the University of California, San Diego, in 1989 with a major in History. In 1993 she received a master's degree in Education from the United States International University and is currently teaching math to seventh- and eighth-graders in San Diego.

Stephanie A. Courtney is a 1992 graduate of the State University of New York at Binghamton. She graduated from the Neighborhood Playhouse School of the Theater in 1994 and is currently an actress living in New York City.

Jaime Dominguez, after graduation from the University of California, San Diego, in 1991, worked as a social services supervisor for Headstart in Los Angeles. In the fall of 1994 he began graduate work toward a Ph.D. in Public Policy Analysis at the University of Illinois–Chicago.

Ann Fenech graduated from the State University of New York at Binghamton in 1992 with a B.A. in English and History. She is currently publications assistant at the State University of New York Press and is studying for an M.A. in English at the State University of New York at Albany.

Gloria Genel graduated from the University of California, San Diego, in 1991 with a B.A. in U.S. History. She is currently employed by the Archdiocese of Los Angeles Education and Welfare Corporation as an employee representative.

Karen A. Gryga graduated from the State University of New York at Binghamton in 1993 with a degree in History and English. She is currently enrolled in the English Education graduate program at Syracuse University.

Raffi Ishkanian grew up in a multicultural setting in Westchester County, New York. As a youth he attended an Armenian church and weekly Armenian language classes. He is currently a student at the State University of New York at Binghamton and has had summer internships with the Armenian General Benevolent Union and Freedom House.

Sang-Hoon Kim is a student at the State University of New York at Binghamton majoring in Biology. He plans to go on to medical school after graduation.

Soo Y. Kim earned her B.A. degree at the State University of New York at Binghamton in 1994 with majors in Biology and History. She is currently working in New York City and planning to attend law school. She has been active in organizations advocating the political empowerment and civil rights of Asian Americans.

Sara Kindler graduated from the State University of New York at Binghamton in 1994 with a major in History. She is planning to work in a field that will permit her to contribute to protecting and preserving the environment.

Michele Kitko earned a B.A. in Psychology from the University of California, San Diego, in 1985. After a period in film and video production, she began working as an elementary school teacher in New York City in 1994. In her spare time she is working on a screenplay and a book.

Rachel Koch graduated from the State University of New York at Binghamton in 1991 with a degree in Psychology. She did graduate study at Northeastern University in Boston and is now working as a school psychologist in Hicksville, New York.

Tanya Mlodzinski graduated from the State University of New York at Binghamton in 1991 and earned a master's in Education in 1992. She is currently teaching fifth grade in Candor, New York.

Anh-Dao Nguyen earned a B.A. degree from the University of California, San Diego, in 1990 in Economics and French. He is employed as a senior buyer by Rohr, a leading aerospace company in San Diego. He plans further graduate study in business and hopes to pursue a career with an American firm doing business in Vietnam.

Cecilia Pineda earned her B.A. degree from the University of California, San Diego, in 1980, with a double major in Communications and Psychology. She received an M.S. degree in Counselor Education at San Diego State University in 1981 and has worked for the University of California for thirteen years, most recently as an associate director of undergraduate admissions at UCLA.

LaToya Powell is an undergraduate at the State University of New York at Binghamton, where she is majoring in English and African American Studies. She plans to teach high school in inner-city schools and eventually to write on subjects such as multiculuralism in education and women of color under siege.

Rose Rameau came to the United States from Haiti in 1989. She graduated in 1994 from the State University of New York at Binghamton with a double major in French and Spanish. She is currently enrolled in a graduate program in French literature at Middlebury College and is studying in France.

Shana R. Rivas graduated from the State University of New York at Binghamton in 1993 and currently resides in Queens, New York, where she is an accounts representative and a prospective M.B.A. candidate. She has adapted to being of black and Puerto Rican heritage, and enjoys living in two cultures.

Lila Shah graduated from the State University of New York at Binghamton in 1992 with a major in Political Science. She hopes to attend medical school and become a physician. Before starting her medical training, she plans to travel in India, where she will work for several months in a clinic for the disadvantaged.

Vladimir Sinayuk came to the United States from Russia in 1976. He graduated from the State University of New York at Binghamton in 1993 with a major in Economics. After graduation he volunteered for ten months in a social service program in Israel. He is interested in a career in international business.

Lynn Sugamura graduated from the University of California, San Diego, in 1987 with a major in Biology. She was listed in *Who's Who among Students in American Universities and Colleges* in 1986. Since graduation she has traveled extensively, including trips to Heart Mountain, Wyoming, where her maternal grandparents and her mother were interned during World War II, and to Japan, where she met relatives on her mother's side.

Catherine Tagudin graduated from the University of California, San Diego, in 1988 with a double major in Psychology and Physiology. In 1992 she earned a doctorate in Optometry. She currently practices optometry in San Diego in a largely Filipino community and is relearning Tagalog with the help of many delighted patients.

Cathy Thompson graduated from the University of California, San Diego, in 1992 with a major in Psychology. She is working toward a Ph.D. in Clinical Psychology, and her dissertation research will focus on identity development of biracial individuals.

Marc Turetzky graduated from the University of California, San Diego, in 1983 and is currently a doctoral candidate in Political Science at Florida State University, focusing on peace studies, international cooperation, and international political economy.

Bob Vaage is a 1979 graduate of the University of California, San Diego, and practices law in San Diego.